By Benjamin R. Epstein

COLD POGROM
(translated from the German)
COLLECTED ESSAYS ON MASARYK
(translated from the German)

By Arnold Forster

ANTI-SEMITISM—1947
A MEASURE OF FREEDOM

By Benjamin R. Epstein
and Arnold Forster

THE TROUBLEMAKERS
CROSS-CURRENTS
SOME OF MY BEST FRIENDS . . .
DANGER ON THE RIGHT
REPORT ON THE KU KLUX KLAN
REPORT ON THE JOHN BIRCH SOCIETY 1966

THE RADICAL RIGHT

Report on the
John Birch Society
and Its Allies

Benjamin R. Epstein
and Arnold Forster

THE
RADICAL
RIGHT

Report on the
John Birch Society
and Its Allies

RANDOM HOUSE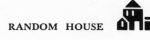

New York

To the Memory of
Adlai E. Stevenson

Democracy itself will always defy definition just because every citizen has a built-in right to formulate definitions of his own.

But today democracy here at home and around the world is being strained and tested as never before. What are the dangers it must overcome? I think on the basis of our own American experience we can begin by disposing of certain imaginary dangers . . . fears, compounded of fact and fiction. . . . From the extreme right we still hear that the income tax is socialism, socialism is communism, and so freedom is already done for. Or we hear that the real threat is not in the truculent power of Moscow or Peking, but in the freedom of unpopular opinion—or in any authority, be it President or Supreme Court, which refuses to punish error as if it were treason.

Or we hear that the United Nations is a big Communist plot. Some plot—to organize all those votes against yourself.

If you follow that line to the end, you conclude with the discovery that the worst danger of all is democracy itself!

What a pity it is that the nerves of even one American should be frazzled with these mythical dangers, when there are so many real and deeper dangers for democracy to face in our time!

—Excerpt from an address given to the Anti-Defamation League of B'nai B'rith on January 14, 1962, in New York City by Ambassador Stevenson on the occasion of the presentation to him of ADL's America's Democratic Legacy Award.

Foreword

This book is a current report on the Radical Right—its activities, spokesmen and schemes. It brings up to date our 1966 *Report on the John Birch Society* and sketches in the Radical Right milieu within which it is operating.

To grasp the meaning of the Radical Right one should understand that its leaders—and their followers—are political and social nihilists. They are "anti" to the point where they would damage society as we know it and government as we have it.

With piety they profess allegiance *for* the Constitution. However, a close examination of their agenda indicates they are *against* the major institutions and social instruments which have been created under the Constitution's benign umbrella. In their mouths the word Constitution becomes an abracadabra to be mumbled but not understood or utilized for the construction of a secure society and a free government.

The road the Radical Rightists travel runs backward in time into a world that never was and hopefully never will be. It is a world in which nothing is ever what it seems. Everything is weighed down by the irresponsibility which grows out of a conspiratorial interpretation of history. Yet the Radical Rightists, in their efforts to stem human progress in our nation, run the gamut from such irresponsibility to the merely perverse.

In such a world it is easy enough to confuse efforts to improve the civil rights of minorities with Red revolution.

The statement that all of Washington and the churches and the schools and the libraries and the Supreme Court are 80% in the hands of Communists becomes an article of faith. Such faith breeds fear and, consequently, a program that calls for the impeachment of the Chief Justice, an end to the fluoridation of water, the ousting of the United Nations from the United States and the condemnation of almost anyone who does not quite agree with these conclusions.

The Radical Rightists are a mixed bag, indeed, each with his own formula for salvation. There are the propagandists, the political activists, the moneymakers. Following them are the kooks, from the gun-toters to the midnight phone callers who, like the Scottish ghoulies, go bump in the night, disturbing with their harassments the sleep of decent citizens. The latter are not the concern of this book.

For Kent Courtney and his "Conservative Society of America," salvation lies in the development of a new Right-Wing third party to displace one of the two present national parties. For the Liberty Lobby it lies in the capture of one of the present parties. For The John Birch Society it lies in the distortion of political thought and the assumption of power by infiltration.

Billy James Hargis, mixing political extremism with religion, likes to travel a gold-lined road; Robert DePugh gets satisfaction out of playing with dynamite (the real thing) even if it should land some of his Minutemen in jail.

For the nation as we know it, that sensible America which travels the democratic road, there will be jeopardy unless it meets the Radical Right's challenge to orderly progress toward social justice for all men.

It is true that America has survived extremist challenges, of Right and Left, in the past—starting with the Salem witch trials of three centuries ago—but not without national pain, temporary damage and deep and sometimes violent conflict. Out of control, the damage can be much more than superficial or temporary.

To check the destructiveness of Radical Rightism, to reduce the damage, to alleviate the pain, every American needs to understand who the Radical Rightists are, what they stand for and how they are proceeding with their divisive tactics.

This book puts their blueprint on record.

DORE SCHARY

Contents

Authors' Acknowledgments

The Radical Right—Report on the John Birch Society and its Allies could not have been prepared without the dedicated efforts of a number of people connected with the Anti-Defamation League of B'nai B'rith at its national headquarters in New York City and its 28 regional offices in strategic locations across the country. The authors are indebted to the many who have contributed to the documentation and analysis of the activities of the Radical Right, and they are most grateful to a handful of people whose individual and collective intelligence helped to shape the final product. Warm thanks are owed to Jerome Bakst, ADL's director of research and evaluation; to Justin J. Finger, director of fact-finding; to Mortimer Kass and Gerald Baumgarten, who so ably assisted in these areas, and especially to J. Q. Purcell, whose editorial counsel was invaluable in pulling it all together.

B. R. E.
A. F.

Part One

THE RADICAL RIGHT

CHAPTER ONE

Recognizing the Danger

The American people, generally cognizant of the real dangers posed on the Left by international Communism, and ready and willing to defend their democratic institutions against its advances, have not been so alert in recognizing the danger on the Right—the threat from those who despise and fear democracy's twentieth century advances and who would tear down the whole American structure in their effort to obliterate the hated changes. This Radical Right, a home-grown extremist movement mushrooming since the beginning of the 1960s, has been carrying on a formidable nationwide propaganda assault on the American mind.

In its massive effort to change American political thinking and turn back the clock of recent history, the Radical Right is tapping, and then pouring out again, many millions of dollars every year. There is no way to pinpoint the exact amount that is spent annually, but careful study of the scope of the extremist propaganda offensive indicates that it is somewhere in the neighborhood of $20,000,000 a year.

The spearhead of the Radical Right movement is The John Birch Society, the large and monolithic organization of self-proclaimed patriots operating through some 4,000 semisecret chapters at the grass-roots level in communities

3

from coast to coast and boasting some 75,000 to 85,000 members spread throughout every state of the Union.

While the Radical Right, viewed as a whole, presents a reactionary spectrum of viewpoints, tactics and fanaticism, the authoritarian Birch Society is its vanguard and its broad base of strength. For the Society has been the primary membership organization of the movement—its backbone and its bellwether.

The Society's strategists and its tightly organized chain of command provide the leadership, and its membership forms the ideological infantry—the foot soldiers—of the Radical Right. Other Rightist organizations complement the Society's effort, creating—via thousands of radio broadcasts and hundreds of rallies, tent shows, political schools, and publications—the ideological climate that aids its grassroots recruitment and extends the impact of the Birchite propaganda effort.

There is a noticeable interlocking of personnel and intertwining of activity between the Birch Society and other Radical Right groups. The leadership levels of many Rightist outfits abound with Birchers. Many such organizations have availed themselves of the services provided by the Society's American Opinion Speakers Bureau, and of the facilities of its more than 350 American Opinion bookstores, which in turn stock and recommend hundreds of books, periodicals, record albums, and tapes issued regularly from all areas of the Right.

This, then, is the essence of the Radical Right's grand assault in the 1960s, an assault that seeks to penetrate every aspect of American life. The picture that emerges, from years of careful observation, is that of a sizeable and well-financed movement that has made significant inroads on America's political and community life.

The hallmark of the phenomenon is everywhere visible: a propaganda theme that sees the United States in the grip of a deeply entrenched, well-advanced internal Communist conspiracy that maintains a stranglehold on the

4

Federal Government, the local town council, the school board, the press, the public library, and the pulpit; that names statesmen and clergymen, editors and teachers, scientists, civil rights leaders, and even singers as traitors and agents of the Great Red Plot. The enemy's works are supposedly to be seen in twentieth century American social progress and in the growing awareness on the part of Americans of world interdependence. And the enemy is based not in Moscow or in Peking, but in Washington—and in the local town hall, school, or church rectory.

Now well entrenched on the American scene, the Radical Right has, since 1964, laid ambitious plans for its future role. The most significant recent developments in its major organizations include:

A greater use of the mass media for propaganda purposes —particularly the wide use of radio broadcasting. An increased emphasis on the potential of activities at the grassroots level. A strong, almost united-front attack on the civil rights movement—as well as stepped-up attacks on the churches and schools as factors in the alleged Communist conspiracy. And possibly most important, an increased emphasis on openly *political* thinking, *political* organization, and *political* action.

In short, the attack from the extremist position is now broad and well integrated, in many areas well financed, and everywhere more determined than ever to achieve success.

5

CHAPTER TWO

The
Radical
Thrust

The chief propaganda vehicle of the assault from the Radical Right is the medium of radio. At least 5,000 broadcasts each week now carry the Radical Right Wing message to various parts of the country.

But the propagandists of the movement have not neglected other media. A complex of publications—weekly newspapers and monthly magazines—give the Radical Right doctrines a circulation well into the hundreds of thousands. The strident voices of extremism are heard on long-playing records and tapes, on the sound tracks of films, and even on the telephone. . . .

Propaganda on the Air

For a great number of Americans the first exposure to the visions and vagaries of the Radical Right comes through the living-room loudspeaker—through the huge patchwork blanket of radio broadcasts that the extremists have put together over the years. In dozens of cities and in hundreds of smaller towns (some of which do not have a daily newspaper of their own), the news is often filtered through the bias of two or three or a half-dozen commentaries by regular party-liners of the Radical Right. Through such commentaries millions of Americans, many of them confused, worried, politically naive, or news-starved in small-town provincialism, are fed a steady diet of propaganda—daily tirades against the civil rights movement, against the United Nations, against the National Council of Churches or the PTA or anti-poverty programs or the income tax.

• More than 600 stations carry the 20th Century Reformation Hour broadcasts of Rev. Carl McIntire, a New Jersey-based fundamentalist churchman who reaches millions with dire warnings against "modernism," and liberalism, as well as attacks on civil rights, labor, and the United Nations. McIntire also is launching broadcasts in the Caribbean area.

• Some 400 stations carry the views of H. L. Hunt, the Texas oil billionaire whose ultra-rightist views are expounded through other, more professional voices on the daily (sometimes twice daily) Life Line programs. Hunt, who claims more than 5,000,000 listeners, refers to those with whom he disagrees, and to all who disagree with him, as "the Mistaken"—with the capital "M" (when it is in print) a slight hint of conspiracy. He also prefers "constructive" to "conservative" in labeling views with which he agrees.

• About 200 stations carry the Manion Forum, the broadcasts of Clarence Manion, a member of the National Council of The John Birch Society.

• Almost 200 stations carry the broadcasts of the Rev. Billy James Hargis, a heavy-set, fiery evangelist of both religious and political fundamentalism whose Tulsa-based Christian Crusade has been one of the major pulpits of the Radical Right in the 1960s—for such speakers as Robert Welch and former Maj. Gen. Edwin A. Walker, as well as Hargis himself. Christian Crusade has also been one of the more lucrative organizations on the Radical Right.

• More than 125 radio and TV outlets carry the Dan Smoot Report. Smoot, a former government agent and once the radio voice for H. L. Hunt, has called at various times through the years for the impeachment of President

7

Kennedy, for U.S. withdrawal from the United Nations, for repeal of the income tax, and for an end to civil rights legislation. He has referred to democracy as "the most evil kind of government possible."

• More than 150 stations carry the broadcasts of the extreme segregationist White Citizens' Councils.

To the above sampling must be added the broadcasts of Edgar C. Bundy, the head of the Church League of America, which peddles dossiers on suspected Communist dupes and sympathizers, and those of Richard Cotten, an undisguised anti-Semite whose 29 outlets in 16 states carry his broadcasts more than 200 times a week. Until recently, Kent Courtney, an arch-segregationist Bircher from New Orleans who heads the Conservative Society of America and leads a perennial Radical Right "third party" political movement was heard on a network of 33 stations.

In January, 1966, after seven years of almost prideful concentration on the printed word, The John Birch Society launched its weekly "Birch Report" broadcasts, offering some recognition to the effectiveness of radio, the chief propaganda medium of its allies. Although it was classified as a minor Society project, by late 1966 the program was being heard on more than 175 radio stations.

The overall wireless attack is often heavily concentrated, in areas where it monopolizes the field of news analysis. One station in Spanish Fork, Utah, has carried the broadcasts of nine Radical Rightists each week—some as often as twice a day. Eleven of them could be heard at various times in any week on one station in Red Lion, Pa.

Powerful stations in Mexico and in San Diego, California, beam many propagandists of the Radical Right over a wide geographical area that covers most of the Western and Southwestern states.

The inevitable result of the saturation in any such community is indoctrination. And for all the "educational" labels usually pinned to the extremists' product, indoctrination *is* the obvious intent of its producers. Obvious,

8

for example, to the chairman of the Democratic National Committee, who has charged ten particular radio stations with flagrant disregard for the Federal Communications Commission's "fairness doctrine" in permitting unanswered political attacks on the Johnson Administration. Specifically named were two Manion Forum broadcasts accusing the State Department of submitting to Communist control. The stations refused to air prepared rebuttals, arguing that since the offending programs had been sponsored, station owners had a responsibility for fairness only if fairness, too, was paid for in cash.

Cash, notably, has been no great problem to Radical Right broadcasters. Most have been able to build up and hold their hundreds of outlets through local sponsorship, small contributions from many listeners, or through the generous gifts of sympathetic foundations. Others have depended upon personal and business wealth; thus Life Line broadcasts have been heavily sponsored by H. L. Hunt's own petroleum and food concerns. Still others have tapped the beneficence of sympathetic commercial interests—such as the Dr. Ross Dog and Cat Food Co., headed by the late D.B. Lewis, a Radical Right activist in his own right who drew his firm into the sponsorship of more than half of Dan Smoot's radio and TV broadcasts and who helped launch Clarence Manion's television operation. Manion, however, has also made use of fundraising letters written for him by more than 700 American industrialists who sent them to their suppliers and to other businessmen and firms, urging financial support of the Manion Forum. It is obvious that fund-raising pressure from big customers in a competitive field is felt keenly by suppliers.

In many areas the verbal assault of the extremists—night after night, slant upon slant—goes largely unanswered. In some cases, station managements are sympathetic to the extremist views, and this has resulted in obvious program imbalance, heavily weighted to starboard.

Periodicals

While radio has been the favored medium of Radical Right groups other than the Birch Society, they also rely heavily on what Birch Society Founder Robert Welch has called "the surer, harder road of education through the printed word." Even those who make the greatest use of the microphone—including Hargis, McIntire, Smoot, Hunt, Courtney, Bundy, and Cotten—publish regular periodicals and each of them can boast a readership high in the thousands.

Such publications reached new circulation peaks during the political fever of 1964. Although some of these slipped back afterward, as could have been expected, the major periodicals appeared to hold much of their new readership. Still other publications showed marked gains that gave new and disturbing dimensions to the extremist thrust. Notable was *Liberty Letter,* a four-pager published by Liberty Lobby, a Washington, D. C., political pressure group, which had tried and then dropped radio broadcasting, but which has emerged since the 1964 election as one of the more significant of America's Radical Right organizations.

Boasting about 15,000 subscribers before the election, *Liberty Letter* reached some 175,000 readers by the end of 1966, and began to exert a degree of political influence on Capitol Hill. Though published by an organization whose leadership and staff includes anti-Semites and individuals maintaining ties with the anti-Semitic and racist demi-worlds, *Liberty Letter* had become, by early 1967, perhaps the most widely read Radical Rightist publication in the country.

The leading periodicals of the movement show the following approximate circulation figures:

Liberty Letter (Liberty Lobby)	175,000
Christian Beacon (McIntire)	84,700

10

Christian Crusade (Hargis)	71,000
American Opinion (Birch Society)	43,000
Dan Smoot Report	31,000
The Citizen (White Citizens' Councils)	30,000
Independent American (Courtney)	25,000
Freedom Magazine	
(Liberty Amendment Committee)	20,000
Life Lines (H. L. Hunt)	10,000

But to gauge the extent of Radical Rightist publishing operations, it is necessary to add to the above the monthly *Bulletin* of The John Birch Society, carefully read by some 75,000 to 85,000 Americans on a regular basis, and also the Society's weekly *Review of the News,* whose circulation, after a year or so in a new and more attractive magazine format, stands at about 5,800.

A number of other publications have amassed substantial readership. Some reflect the section of Protestant fundamentalism that often finds political expression in Rightist radicalism. One example is *The Defender,* which boasted a circulation of better than 80,000 early in 1966, and more recently claimed 130,000.

Reflecting a Catholic radicalism of the Right is *The Wanderer,* published weekly in St. Paul, with a circulation of about 35,000.

The Councilor, shrilly racist and anti-Semitic periodical of the White Citizens' Councils of Louisiana, had some 60,000 readers early in 1966.

Recordings

In recent years, most of the leading organizations of the Radical Right have begun offering lists of recordings—LP albums or tapes—available either for sale or rental.

Billy James Hargis makes available the recorded speeches of the huge roster of Far Right-thinking personalities who have addressed his annual Christian Crusade conventions.

11

Dr. Fred Schwarz of the Christian Anti-Communism Crusade lists lectures on tape. And recently The John Birch Society has begun to offer for sale record albums with Founder Robert Welch expounding the approved Birchite mythology.

While none of the leading Radical Right organizations itself overlooks sales possibilities, commercial recording firms have seen the purely cash potential of the Far Rightist market and have begun catering to this audience. One commercial enterprise—Key Records, in California, headed by Vick Knight—has developed a long list of recordings, featuring well-known leaders and personalities of the Far Right, including Tom Anderson, a member of The John Birch Society's National Council and a favorite orator and "humorist" of the starboard fringe. One speech, which Anderson has delivered "live" before many audiences, bears the title *Bipartisan Treason*. It is a jocular, capsulized summary of the extremist view of recent national Administrations, Republican and Democratic alike. Since the platter was cut, the faithful who heard Anderson deliver it in person can relive the great moment; those who didn't can hear it for the first time, postage paid.

Another development during 1966 was the appearance of a Conservative Record-of-the-Month Club, with headquarters in Lynwood, Calif. An advertisement in September, 1966, said the club was "designed for you, the patriotic-minded individual, who, each month, will receive in record form, the most powerful weapon against the Communist conspiracy—KNOWLEDGE." One major offering: *The True Story of Civil Rights,* featuring Alan Stang, author of a basic Birch Society text on the civil rights movement as a Communist manifestation.

Poison on the Telephone

A relatively new wrinkle in the extremists' overall propaganda system is the use of the telephone.

12

The telephone company's automatic recorded message service, which makes it possible for anyone dialing a given number to hear a taped message, has been used for the dissemination of weather reports, the time of day, baseball scores, and even prayers. In 1962, Dr. William Campbell Douglass, a Sarasota, Fla., physician and an avowed member of the Birch Society, discovered the message service as a viable medium for disseminating the message of the Radical Right. By the end of 1966, he had set up more than 100 outlets, including in the service all of America's major cities. Anyone living near an outlet could, by dialing a well-advertised local number, hear a 60- to 90-second "educational" lecture from the most extreme schools of thought.

Dr. Douglass's operation is called Let Freedom Ring.

Each of his subscribing "stations" receives from Sarasota, for $24 a year, a weekly script to be read by a local voice onto the machine's tape. (The machines are rented from the telephone company by the local sponsors.) The recorded voice may speak of "treason right in the White House"—naming the President himself as a traitor—or may launch into similar attacks on the churches, on the schools, or on civil rights leaders. For many years, in many cities, the voice was completely unidentified, hiding its slanders in anonymity.

Let Freedom Ring has called such anonymity an exercise of the right of privacy, its "stations" technically holding unlisted numbers. Thus have many of the voices of fear and suspicion avoided any semblance of public responsibility for their assaults.

In 1965, the National Council of Churches and the Anti-Defamation League of B'nai B'rith filed complaints with the Federal Communications Commission against the use of telephone anonymity in "abusive and extremist attacks on individuals and organizations." Not long afterward, at hearings before a Senate subcommittee, Dr. Douglass protested that if legislation requiring identification of local LFR sponsors were passed, his local entrepreneurs would be harassed by "Leftists." Nonetheless, the telephone companies eventually agreed to disclose the sponsors of such "stations" upon request and to require that the name and address of each outlet be plainly stated in each recording. (Policing apparently became difficult. The requirement was met on at least a few LFR outlets by the naming of Let Freedom Ring and a post office box number, with postal anonymity taking over as a new barrier against complete identification.)

The LFR messages are reaching a growing public. Between 1964 and 1966, Let Freedom Ring became one of the fastest growing interests of local Radical Right "activists" in many a city and town. Moreover, the idea caught on with other organizations. The White Citizens' Councils have for some time operated a similar phone message "station" in New Orleans. The John Birch Society has tried it in several areas. In the New Jersey town of Summit, the Society's own automated propaganda voice has emanated from the same basement room as that of Let Freedom Ring's local outlet.

The advantages of LFR's gimmick, and its early adoption of the Birch ideology in the broad, reckless nature of its "anti-Communism," has drawn Dr. Douglass's telephone network into close cooperation with members of The John Birch Society in many of its 100 cities. The LFR scripts have often recommended the Society's publications and have suggested that they be purchased through Robert Welch's Belmont, Mass., headquarters. Many Society members and many of the Society's American Opinion bookstores have been listed as holders of the official addresses of Let Freedom Ring stations. In Dedham, Mass., moreover, an employee of the Birch Society's headquarters in nearby Belmont was broadcasting the local LFR messages from his home. LFR's New Orleans box number was registered in the name of the *Independent American,* published by Birch-liner Phoebe Courtney.

Other "stations" in other localities gradually became

14

prime local projects of the Society's activists. The number of Let Freedom Ring outlets across the country more than doubled between September, 1965, and September, 1966. Apparently, many thousands of curious callers had begun to lend an ear—as well as the undivided attention usually accorded the voice on the telephone—to the feverish pitch of the extreme Right.

CHAPTER THREE

The Propaganda Line

The battle cry of the Radical Right is a call for the repeal of the social progress of many years. It is a chorus of oversimple answers to complex problems, and a demand for quick "victories" in today's tangled and dangerous world struggles. It is shouts and whispers of treason in high places and charges that the Communist conspiracy controls the United States of America.

It is an assault on our greatest national institutions and a constant round of sniping attacks on the local level. And it is almost purely negative—with more accusations than answers.

Less than successful in beclouding our national purposes, the propaganda of the Radical Right has all too often succeeded in shredding the integrity of a single community and in fattening local Birch Society chapters with the convinced, the confused, and the fearful.

The trademark of the propaganda line is its assumption of a conspiracy theory of history—the theory that a secret, diabolical, "Communist" claque actually plans and executes the major events affecting our personal and national destinies. This assumption pervades the extremist line of thinking. (A distinction must be made between these conspiracy theorists of the Radical Right and those extreme conservatives who hold that the foreign policies and domestic programs they abhor are the products of liberal blindness, stupidity, bungling, and chicanery, rather than the work of secret international plotters.)

The bizarre possibilities of the conspiracy theory become reality in Radical Right publications and at Radical Right rallies, tent meetings, and conventions. For example, in the speeches of the Rev. David Noebel, a preacher with Billy James Hargis's Christian Crusade who "reveals," as Crusade flyers declare, "the Communist infiltration of American youth by means of a long-range, systematic plan to sabotage American culture, religion and beliefs through the use of music being 'fed' children from two through their teens!"

The author of two recent books, *Rhythm, Riots, and Revolution,* and *Communism, Hypnotism and the Beatles,* Noebel names that phenomenally successful English singing group as, in the Crusade's words, "part of a systematic plan geared to making a generation of American youth mentally ill and emotionally unstable." This is being done, he said, by timing musical rhythms to the actual physical pulse-beat of the teenager, thus anaesthetizing the control centers of his brain, demoralizing and destroying him.

Billy James Hargis himself subscribes to the theory of a great conspiracy, and has named its chief American agents:

> There is a master conspiracy loose in the world today headed by Satan himself . . .
>
> In the field of religion, the satanic conspiracy uses the National Council of Churches . . .
>
> In the field of education, the satanic conspiracy uses the National Education Association . . .
>
> In the field of politics, the satanic conspiracy uses the Americans for Democratic Action . . .
>
> In the field of race relations, the satanic conspiracy uses the National Association for the Advancement of Colored People . . .

The satanic conspirators, though allegedly guided from Below, are usually the Communists, or the "socialist world planners." Along this line, Billy James Hargis made a

17

dramatic announcement in a letter dated September 14, 1965:

> I have frightening information concerning a diabolical plan for U.S. disarmament and abolition of U.S. sovereignty by 1976 listing specific dates of future wars, assassinations, etc., outlined in a 54-page contract between the Air Force and North American Aviation which has just come into my hands . . .

The document had "come into" Hargis's hands through one Bill Manahan, an Anaheim, Calif., scientist employed at the aviation plant. It allegedly prophesies events of the next ten years "deliberately manufactured by the two governments involved" (the United States and the USSR) to bring about "world control." Manahan, a member of the Christian Crusade, had "leaked" copies of the contract to Republican Sen. Strom Thurmond of South Carolina and Republican Rep. James Utt of California, to "Americans for National Security," a Rightist pressure group linked closely with Liberty Lobby, and to The John Birch Society. (Early in 1967, Manahan was one of four new special field representatives named to the staff of Christian Crusade's Development Department.)

The contract actually delineated a series of hypothetical world events dreamed up for the use of intellectual "think factories" in their effort to come up with answers that might be helpful to the Air Force in planning future defense requirements. (A clue to the hypothetical or even fictional nature of the events should have been obvious: the document's poor "predictions." It stated, for example, that Indonesia would explode a nuclear device by the fall of 1965.)

Hargis, however, managed to frighten a lot of people, as he probably did also with the publication of another newsletter in which he asked:

"Is Fidel Castro the Mastermind Behind American Negro Revolution?"

During a lengthy answer, the Tulsa evangelist stated unequivocally (emphasis his): *"The rebellion in Santo Domingo, and the one in Los Angeles can be easily identified as part of one great big Communist plot."*

It is not always easy to determine (as it was in the case of the "frightening" Air Force contract) the sources of Rightist prophecy.

"Secret but very reliable sources" were credited by former counterspy Herbert A. Philbrick when he told a rally, sponsored by the traveling Christian Anti-Communism Crusade in Garden City, N.Y., in the fall of 1965, that the Communists were planning violent riots in 20 American cities on the 15th and 16th of October. The disturbances were to be, he warned, "twenty Berkeleys—twenty Los Angeleses—all at one time." And, as usually happens in the exciting life on the Radical Right, little was remembered of his words only a few weeks later, when the dreaded days of mid-October came and went without incident.

In the case of such nonexistent terrors, and with real ones also, it is an almost automatic reflex on the part of Radical Right propagandists to see the hand of the Communist conspiracy at work. This illusion has become, in the extremism of the 1960s, a fantasy to dwarf the nightmares of the McCarthyites in the 1950s. Today, charges of treason are made not against government clerks or army dentists, but against the highest officials in Washington, including Presidents of the United States. (Oilman H. L. Hunt makes an interesting commentary: "Officials are becoming irate with charges made by those opposing Communists," he wrote in his widely-distributed newspaper column. "If the officials are nearly or completely innocent, they will not be injured by false charges made against them." And so much for the subject of false charges.)

Clarence Manion sweeps wide with statements like: "With the unwitting help of our modern Liberal leadership, Communism has now taken all but complete command of mankind."

19

Early in 1966, Dr. Fred Schwarz, the Australian-born physician who leads the Christian Anti-Communism Crusade, spoke—almost in rebuttal of Manion—of "the significant setbacks communism has suffered during 1965 in many areas of the world." But he also mentioned the "obvious progress made by the Communists within the United States during the same period."

The Radical Right's projection of the map colors the United States brightly pink in a world shaded deeply red. And its definition of "Communism" is as broad as the brush used for smearing. Something called "The Committee" in Miami Shores, Fla. (using a post office box formerly listed under The John Birch Society), found that even cigarette-smoking may be hazardous to national security. Certain American brands, the group declared, are made from:

"COMMUNIST TOBACCO."

At Christmas time, 1966, Let Freedom Ring, charging that one major tobacco company was buying tobacco from Yugoslavia, attacked the American Legion for accepting advertising in its magazine from the offending company. "The American Legion," the message said, "*used* to fight Communism with its every fiber. But now these Communist-supporting cigarettes are actually advertised in the American Legion magazine."

The episode proved what students of the Radical Right had long been saying—that no one, no individual, organization or publication, no matter how patriotic or how conservative, is safe from the wrath of the extremists of the Radical Right.

Little, if anything, is labeled in the Radical Right lexicon as merely bad, ill-advised, or in error. It is always *Red,* and darkly conspiratorial. The War on Poverty, cried the telephone voices of Let Freedom Ring, is "a government-financed training ground for Communist revolutionaries." The United Nations, they declared, is "an instrument of Communist policy." Even teachers' associations and the League of Women Voters have been brushed with Red by LFR's "stations."

And if seeing conspirators behind everything they dislike seems a major preoccupation of the Radical Right, it is possible that this is simply because they dislike so many things.

The "Anti-" Complex

One does not properly toe the Radical Rightist line unless one speaks out vociferously against the UN, the civil rights movement, mental health programs, the National Council of Churches, federal aid to schools, The Anti-Defamation League, *The New York Times,* disarmament treaties, and the fluoridation of water. Some carry their dislike even further.

Billy James Hargis has described President Johnson, the Congress, and the courts of our country as "anti-Christ."

On American trade with eastern European nations, New York's Let Freedom Ring outlet declared that "for the first time in our history, a President has openly advocated treason as a national policy."

Another of the weekly telephone messages accused the President of "trading with our Communist enemies while attacking with all the savagery of a Barbary pirate our friends in Rhodesia." (Through 1965-66, many on the Radical Right became avid supporters of Rhodesian white supremacists.)

"Lyndon Johnson," cried another of LFR's anonymous speakers, "will go down in history as Mr. Surrender."

But all is not "anti-" on the Let Freedom Ring phone circuits. One recorded message, indicating something Dr. Douglass's operation was *for,* asked:

"What's wrong with The John Birch Society?"

Much of the extremists' "anti-" position is justified, or at least rationalized, by a strongly "pro-" stand on the United States Constitution—though on a very literal, fundamentalist interpretation of it, to be sure. But their support does not extend to the judicial body that interprets the Constitution—namely, the United States Supreme Court. Decisions of that tribunal distasteful to the Radical Right are seen as evidence that the Communist conspiracy has penetrated to the nation's highest court. Important rulings are met by the cry, "Impeach Earl Warren!" or the question, asked rhetorically by Mississippi's Sen. James O. Eastland, and widely circulated by the Birch Society: "Is the Supreme Court pro-Communist?"

The Birchers are not alone in seeking the impeachment of the Chief Justice of the United States, an "agenda" item in their *Bulletins* each month. Dan Smoot, in his *Report,* called for such action early in 1965. Billy James Hargis, in a pamphlet entitled *Six Men Against God,* declared:

> In the past, I was cautious concerning these projects to impeach Earl Warren. Now it is my earnest conviction that ever [*sic*] member of the United States Supreme Court who either voted to outlaw prayer in the public schools, or was a party to this decision by silence should be impeached.

In reply to the charge that they present a negative image through their "anti-" positions, the Far Rightists can point to their unanimous support *for* the so-called Liberty Amendment—a proposed Constitutional amendment requiring that the Federal Government "get out of private business" (Social Security, atomic energy, banking, army construction, veterans' insurance, national forests, TVA, etc.), and sell such enterprises to private owners. Such a course, supporters claim, would result in a reduction in government costs sufficient to make the federal income tax unnecessary—and so the second part of the proposed Liberty Amendment calls for the abolition of this tax.

The Liberty Amendment (it has already passed in the legislatures of seven states) would, of course, virtually dismantle the United States Government. Thus, Radical Right support for the Amendment—it is a standard Birch Society agenda item—is perhaps not so positive a position after all.

The Liberty Amendment's originator and constant advocate, Willis E. Stone, himself reflects the negativism of most Radical Right thinking. His view of the United States in 1966:

"A subservient Congress, a bewildered people, and an administration apparently eager to abandon every historic American precept" and bring about "the thorough subjugation of the American people."

Attacks on the Churches

Perhaps the most consistent target of the Radical Right's negative propaganda has been the churches—particularly when they espouse social applications of Christian teaching. For a large and vocal segment of the extreme Right Wing in America consists of religious fundamentalists who distrust the social gospel, ecumenism, and sometimes Roman Catholicism.

Protestantism's National Council of Churches, however, has borne the brunt of the attacks. The NCC has been the special target of the Reverends Billy James Hargis and Carl McIntire, of Myers G. Lowman, head of the fundamentalist Circuit Riders, Inc., and even of the peripatetic former Maj. Gen. Edwin A. Walker, military hero of the Birch Society and its allies.

Hargis, who argues that his Christian Crusade does not believe in name-calling or character-assassination, has recently described the National Council of Churches as an apologist for Communism, a collaborator with Communists, and a supporter of immorality and race riots.

"The National Council of Churches of Christ," Hargis italicized, *"is the instrument being used by Satan and his followers* to apostasize the Protestant churches of Jesus Christ."

Hargis's advertisement for his books attacking the NCC

has a bright red hammer-and-sickle superimposed on it. The title of one classic Hargis pamphlet, already in at least six printings, charges the NCC with *50 Counts of Treason to God and Country.*

Myers G. Lowman assails contemporary churchmen for their interest in civil rights and social causes. He is the author of several compilations purporting to show the pro-Communist associations and affiliations of clergymen of various faiths. One of these is *A Compilation of Public Records of 658 Clergymen and Laymen Connected With the National Council of Churches,* which has been sold in some Birch Society bookstores. Like many on the Radical Right, Lowman does not always seem able to distinguish between liberal causes and those that are Communist or pro-Communist. Indications that the activities of his Circuit Riders, Inc., cannot be viewed as purely religious or educational came recently when the Internal Revenue Service revoked its tax-exempt status.

Former Maj. Gen. Edwin A. Walker, a hero of the extremists for almost five years, told an audience at Charleston, S.C., in September, 1965, that the National Council of Churches "is a front for the Catholic Church and the Catholic Church is a front for the National Council of Churches." At the 1965 convention of Hargis' Christian Crusade in Los Angeles, Walker urged the audience to stop putting money in church collection baskets on Sundays, to send it instead to the Crusade's Tulsa headquarters.

(A similar stand was taken by Christians Against Atheistic Communism, a local Chicago group, during the summer of 1966, when racial tensions ran high. CAAC, led by David Sheehan, an avowed Bircher, distributed flyers advising "thinking citizens who want law, order, and neighborhood peace" to refrain from placing "their money in offering baskets passed in the churches connected with the Chicago Archdiocese or the Church Federation of Greater Chicago." The flyers also denounced Roman Catholic Archbishop John Cody as sympathetic to civil rights leaders viewed as pro-Communist by CAAC. A year earlier, Sheehan had picketed a dinner given for the Archbishop when the latter assumed his ecclesiastical duties in Chicago.)

The fountainhead of propaganda aimed at discrediting the National Council of Churches is the Rev. Carl McIntire of Collingswood, N.J. From that quiet suburb in the Philadelphia-Camden area, McIntire presides over a huge complex of organizations and activities—including the American Council of Christian Churches (formed to oppose the NCC), the 20th Century Reformation Hour broadcasts over some 600 stations, and the weekly *Christian Beacon,* with a circulation of 84,700. The McIntire complex, one of the more successful operations on the Radical Right, has an annual gross estimated in the millions.

McIntire has branded the National and World Councils of Churches as "cooperating fronts for World Socialism." Because of the National Council's dedication to the cause of civil rights for Negroes, he has charged that the great Protestant body was "becoming a companion of riotous men and a shame to Christianity." A 1965 letter sent out by Marion H. Reynolds, Jr., president of McIntire's own church council, labeled the NCC "the enemies of faith and freedom."

In addition to his obvious hatred for "modern" Protestantism, Rev. Carl McIntire harbors little good will toward the Roman Catholic Church. He has a record of anti-Catholicism and of association with anti-Catholic bigots —such as the late Rev. Harvey Springer, publisher of *Western Voice,* who addressed many McIntire gatherings until his death in 1966.

On the recent visit of His Holiness Pope Paul VI to the United States, McIntire wrote:

> Pope Paul's visit to the United Nations has stunned and shocked conservatives all over the land . . .
> . . . his call for disarmament, his plan for dealing with the poor of the whole world. He had nothing whatever to say about the Communists . . .

It all seems so startling, so stunning, so fantastic.
. . . The Pope has turned out to be a political liberal
. . . He has given the Reds a great victory!

And then came the hints of dark conspiracy:

. . . Just as the UN is to be unique and universal in
the political world, rising to become a world government,
the Roman Catholic Church is to become unique and
universal in the religious world, rising to become the
great ecumenical one-world superchurch.
. . . Surely, my friends, those of you who know something about prophecies can realize that the coming of
the Lord is at hand.

Another New Jersey Radical Right propagandist has
also joined in the discovery of conspiracies in the churches.
He is Frank A. Capell of Zarephath, a pamphleteer who
describes himself as a "traditionalist conservative, fundamentalist Roman Catholic." Capell was one of a group
involved in recent years in the circulation of materials
libeling Republican Senator Thomas Kuchel of California.
The author of such sensationalist booklets as *Treason is
the Reason, The Strange Death of Marilyn Monroe* (charging Communist hanky-panky), and *The Strange Case of
Jacob Javits,* Capell began in 1966 to issue a special bi-
weekly "religious news edition" of his regular four-pager,
Herald of Freedom. The "infiltration of the Christian
religions by the Conspiracy" is Capell's concern and, like
the Circuit Riders' Myers Lowman, Capell is a lister of
names with alleged Far Left associations.

Sometimes, the Radical Right line employs the intem-
perate, doom-filled language found so effective in raising
both blood pressures and funds for extremist crusades.
William Loeb's ultra-conservative daily newspaper, the
Manchester, N.H., *Union Leader,* often reprints the tracts
of propagandists even farther to the Right than itself,
and headlined its reprint (February 15, 1966) of a broad-

cast by Birch Society National Council member Clarence Manion:

"Liberals Launch Pagan Terror—Sundown of Christianity?"

The Local Scene

The brunt of the Radical Right attack on basic American institutions comes at the community level. A leading battlefield is the field of education; the focal point of community culture often becomes the showplace of its prejudices and fanaticisms.

Such was recently the case in Castro Valley, California, where activists demanded that *JB,* by Archibald MacLeish, and *Lord of the Flies,* by William Golding, be removed from an optional reading list for high school seniors. At the same time the district was flooded with unsigned literature implying that the school board's president had Communist connections. The community's Far Rightists imported former government informant Karl Prussion, who has a following among the Radical Rightist fringe, to speak at a local rally. Without mentioning Castro Valley, Prussion spoke on "How the Communists Plan to Take Over Our Schools." Few missed the implication.

Also targets of frequent attacks are community mental health programs, which extremists have charged are part of a Marxist plot to "brainwash" the American people into accepting an atheistic "one-world" state. One of the earlier salvoes was the attack on the Alaska Mental Health Bill of the 1950s, a bill designed to provide the Territory with adequate mental hospitals. Various Radical Right pamphleteers saw the proposed legislation as creating a "concentration camp" for the imprisonment of anti-Communist "patriots," and this theme has recurred in their propaganda for nearly a decade.

In Dallas, in 1964, extremist telephone calls and fright mail caused some volunteer collectors to drop out of the

27

mental health fund campaign. A fashion show held to provide psychiatric equipment for a proposed children's medical center was nearly wrecked when a group of Radical Rightists convinced a leading Dallas department store to withdraw its support; a woman had presented the management with a petition signed by 100 customers and bearing a clear threat of canceling all future business.

The nationwide propaganda behind local attacks on mental health programs has poured at various times from The John Birch Society, the *Dan Smoot Report,* the Manion Forum, and the White Citizens' Councils. It has been written by individuals such as John Stormer (in *None Dare Call It Treason*—a Far Right paperback which sold millions of copies during the 1964 Presidential election campaign), and Billy James Hargis, who has said that "Christians appear to be a major target of the mental health promoters."

While the Rightist assault wrought havoc in the mental health drive in Dallas in 1964, the following year that city's "patriotic" propaganda network failed to convince the citizenry of the alleged evils in the fluoridation of water. A public referendum approved the use of fluoride in the city's water by three to one—while various dismayed far-outers still screamed that it was all a "Communist plot" to infect the public with an "insidious poison."

The letters columns of daily newspapers, open always to the public for unsolicited opinions, have become a major medium for extremist axe-grinding. In many communities these columns are a virtual monopoly of the Far Right Wing. And the letters from that source are invariably long, detailed paraphrases of Radical Right propaganda.

A painstaking study of the subject by a team of University of Michigan political scientists was published in the August, 1965, issue of *American Political Science Review* and reported in the *Wall Street Journal.* The study disclosed that "the large bulk of letters to public officials or the printed media come from a tiny fraction of the population, which tends to write very repetitively," and that this core of almost compulsive letter-writers tended to be oriented toward a distinct Right Wing view.

Some Dare Call It Treason

An important new tool of the Radical Right in recent years—new at least as a *mass* propaganda device—is the medium of book publishing. Shortly before the 1964 Presidential election, the Rightist movement discovered in mass-distributed books a sensational new means of disseminating their propaganda line, as well as—for the Birch Society in particular—an implement for the recruiting of new members. Many of the books distributed at first were thinly disguised political tracts rushed into print in an effort to help defeat President Johnson at the polls.

Perhaps the best-known and most widely distributed was Stormer's *None Dare Call It Treason*, which, some estimates said, reached a distribution of more than 7,000,000 copies and which brought the conspiracy theory of history to a tremendous number of Americans—many of them for the first time. The John Birch Society played a major role in disseminating the book.

Perhaps because the Radical Right's storehouses were glutted with unsold copies, new techniques were devised by some groups to put Stormer's paperback summary of the conspiracy theory into the hands of still other thousands of Americans after the Presidential election campaign was over.

During 1965, the California-based Americanism Educational League announced an essay contest for college students based on a reading of Stormer's book. The educational league, headed by Dr. John R. Lechner, who some years ago was listed as a lecturer available through the

Birch Society's speakers' bureau, launched a campaign for $125,000 to supply half a million free copies of the paperback to collegians. (Lechner died in February, 1967.)

Cooperating with the Americanism Educational League was Constructive Action, Inc., of La Jolla, Calif., which has emerged as one of the more active, well-financed and energetic transmission belts for Radical Right propaganda.

During 1964, Constructive Action, whose main moving spirit is Ted Loeffler, its Secretary-Treasurer, handled distribution of more than 2,000,000 copies of Stormer's book, and more than 600,000 copies of two other Rightist paperbacks.

In 1965, as part of the essay contest for collegians, Constructive Action distributed 450,000 of the Stormer books and 150,000 copies of *Slightly to the Right,* written by H. L. Richardson, a former Birch Society coordinator.

Constructive Action was also the producer of a film strip called *Civil Riots, U.S.A.* which has been shown throughout the country before Radical Rightist audiences and which has even been shown by some unsuspecting but respectable groups. The film strip, a Birchite version of the 1965 Watts riot, attributed the disorder to Communist influence and agitation. Constructive Action said some 600 prints were available for such gatherings.

The organization's activities were stepped up during 1966, with college students a continuing target audience. As part of its drive, Constructive Action distributed to students at 60 colleges (those which a majority of the members of the U.S. Congress had attended) a variety of materials, which included 50,000 copies of *You Can Trust the Communists (to be Communists)* by Dr Fred Schwarz of the Christian Anti-Communism Crusade and 20,000 copies of *It's Very Simple* by Alan Stang, an attack on the civil rights movement (as "Communist") published by Western Islands, the Birch Society's book publishing arm.

Another 1966 project of Constructive Action was the production and distribution of 250,000 copies of a book called *Pass the Poverty Please* by Patty Newman in collaboration with Joyce Wenger—an attack leveled at the War on Poverty.

But far more ambitious and ominous was Constructive Action's effort, late in 1966, to mount a saturation propaganda campaign to exploit the fears felt by many Americans about the "black power" slogan advanced by two of the smaller organizations on the civil rights scene.

Constructive Action aimed at bringing to 25,000,000 American families by direct mail, and to 60,000,000 readers by newspaper advertising, a propaganda production of text and pictures highlighting the uglier aspects of some of the riots in the Negro ghettos across the country.

During the fall of 1966, the direct mail version began to show up across the country. Some copies were sent out via addressing plates that bore a striking resemblance to plates used to mail *The Councilor,* the shrill, anti-Semitic and racist propaganda organ of the White Citizens' Councils of Louisiana.

Constructive Action's "black power" propaganda effort bore a handy coupon to aid readers in sending contributions to the La Jolla, Calif., headquarters. Despite the appeal for funds, the organization is already well-financed and has become a major channel for the distribution of Radical Right and Birchite propaganda materials.

During 1966, there was further evidence that the Radical Right was far from finished with Stormer's book. In the summer, a Long Beach, Calif., firm offered 10,000 copies of *None Dare Call It Treason* at a nickel a copy—$5 per carton of 100 copies. Earlier, a group of activists in Las Vegas included copies of Stormer's book in bundles being sent to American troops in Vietnam as part of a "Loot from Las Vegas" project. Commenting on the divisive nature of the book, especially in the hands of fighting troops at the front line, the Las Vegas *Sun* said editorially that "slipping it into the shipment is dangerously near the definition of what an act of treason is."

Authors and Critics

There is little doubt that the age of the paperback book is giving the Radical Right a whole new pipeline for pumping their doctrines into the national consciousness. Few of these paperbacks achieve the mass readership attained by Stormer's flight of fancy, but certainly there is no shortage of Rightist authors, and if they are not reaching millions of readers, their sales figures compare favorably with those of popular books on the national best-seller lists. Most of the Radical Right paperbacks, of course, circulate among the more dedicated members of the extreme fringe, but often the zealous efforts of the faithful bring such books into the homes of Americans who are not part of the movement—and here recruiting begins.

A leading title among the paperbacks during 1965 was *Strike from Space,* by Phyllis Schlafly and retired Rear Adm. Chester Ward, which developed the theme that the Soviets had been developing orbital missiles to strike at the United States from outer space, that the United States was in the meantime disarming unilaterally, and that the Vietnam war was a diversion engineered by the Russians to divert American attention from the Soviets' crash space program.

In 1966, a special "Congressional campaign edition" with supplemental material was rushed into print in time for the Congressional elections. In an interview with Clarence Manion, on the Manion Forum broadcast, Admiral Ward agreed that the essential message of the 1966 edition was "Get rid of McNamara"—this to be accomplished by electing a Congress that would force the Defense Secretary's replacement.

The Schlafly-Ward book received an enthusiastic send-off from the Hargis Christian Crusade and from Liberty Lobby. It was treated less than kindly, however, by the

Birch Society, convinced as the Society is that Communism is primarily an *internal* threat.

The alleged unilateral disarmament of the United States was also treated in *The Phoenix Papers,* by Dr. James Bales of Harding College. The book was promoted by a four-page display advertisement in Hargis' *Christian Crusade* magazine shortly after it became available.

Victory Denied, by Maj. Arch Roberts, a former aide to Maj. Gen. Edwin A. Walker, was sharply critical of the UN, of the alleged "muzzling" of the military by Washington politicians, and of all opponents of Gen. Walker.

Edgar Bundy of the Church League of America brought out *Apostles of Deceit*—an attack on the National Council of Churches and other dangerous "liberal" influences.

Mary Davison, a prolific author who contends that the eminently respectable Council on Foreign Relations is in fact a group of prominent people plotting America's doom, brought out *The Profound Revolution,* an attack on the UN.

Civil rights formed the subject of *The Bondage of the Free* by Kent Steffgen, who has been employed both by the John Birch Society and the White Citizens' Councils. On the same subject, Liberty Lobby sent to every member of Congress a copy of *Open Occupancy vs. Forced Housing Under the Fourteenth Amendment* by Alfred Avins, who has been active in the movement on behalf of "freedom of choice" for Americans to discriminate on racial grounds.

The Patrick Henry Press, a Radical Right segregationist organization based in Richmond, Va., chose teachers and PTAs as target audiences and mailed out half a million copies of a booklet called *How Classroom Desegregation Will Work* by Dr. Henry E. Garrett of Charlottesville, Va., former head of the Psychology Department at Columbia University. The booklet claimed that classroom desegregation couldn't work because the Negro is inferior biologically —hereditarily immature, in Garrett's words. The editor of

Patrick Henry Press is John Synon, long active as a speaker and pamphleteer in Rightist circles. Synon said he hoped to get another 500,000 copies of the Garrett booklet into the mails by the end of 1966.

A sequel to the Garrett argument that "the Negro race is less advanced in an evolutionary sense than is the white race, by perhaps 200,000 years," was on the Patrick Henry presses before the year was out. The second Garrett tract was entitled *Breeding Down,* and claimed that miscegenation can destroy the white race.

Occasionally, Radical Rightist authors use the format of the novel to deliver their propagandistic messages. Dr. Douglass, the founder of Let Freedom Ring, gave the world a bizarre and futuristic little fantasy called *The Eagle's Feather,* which was published in 1966 by Free Men Speak, Inc., the New Orleans publishing operation founded by Kent and Phoebe Courtney.

Described on its red jacket as "a gripping novel of international political intrigue—set in the 1970s," Dr. Douglass' little opus told the story of how Warren Silverbright, an opportunistic Jew, became President of the United States and then acquiesced to an effort to turn the country over to a brutal, Communist-controlled, African-dominated United Nations. In this he was aided by his younger brother, Robbie, a ruthless opportunist ("his hair falling over his boyish face . . .") who rises to Attorney General of the United States and who works with the Communists.

By the middle of the book, President Silverbright has surrendered part of Texas and part of Florida to Communist blackmailers who use his wife's infidelities as a weapon. He then has a change of heart. This ends his usefulness to the Communists, who assassinate him. The assassination is investigated by a Whitehead Commission, headed by a justice of the U.S. Supreme Court.

The country is, in the end, saved from the Reds by the exertions of superpatriots, headed by the hero of the book,

Dr. Dwight Huckins, who operates a telephone grapevine much like Douglass' own Let Freedom Ring. Religious inspiration is given to the patriots by Rev. Bobby Tim Hadley, described as "pink-cheeked and rotund" and more than slightly resembling Billy James Hargis of the Christian Crusade.

There are other themes and characters that remind the reader of today's Radical Right.

A superpatriotic general resigns his position in the armed forces after his activities lead to an investigation—which immediately brings to mind the case of former Maj. Gen. Edwin A. Walker, who resigned from the U.S. Army in 1962 after his "Pro-Blue" troop indoctrination program became a *cause célèbre* in Washington.

An implied bit of praise for the real-life Minutemen organization, which has formed guerrilla-type bands to resist a fancied Communist takeover of the United States, occurs when the hero, Dr. Huckins, declares that some good can come from the loss of Hawaii to the enemy during Silverbright's administration. "The people of the other forty-nine states," the reader learns, "ignoring gun-registration laws, began quietly to arm themselves."

(The story of a Jewish President ready to hand over the United States to the Communist conspiracy was not Dr. Douglass' only recent excursion to the borders of subtle anti-Semitism. Early in 1967, the Let Freedom Ring network carried a message which charged that LSD—the hallucinatory drug—was being smuggled into the United States from Israel, where it was allegedly being manufactured by the Chaim Weizmann Institute. The message said it was all part of the Communist conspiracy designed to immobilize American cities. A spokesman for the institute, one of the largest scientific institutions in the world, said there was "not a scintilla of truth in the outrageous broadcast." The source of the LFR message apparently was the August 12, 1966, issue of Capell's *Herald of Free-*

dom which carried the reference to the Weizmann Institute and which was sent to LFR listeners who wrote in asking for material on the "LSD Conspiracy" offered by LFR.)

The Line on Civil Rights

For years, the Radical Right has carried out a blitzkrieg of propaganda against the civil rights movement and its leaders—lumping responsible civil rights advocates with radical extremists, and branding all without distinction as servants of the Communist conspiracy.

Robert Welch of The John Birch Society seemed to lay down the line in a 16-page pamphlet, *Two Revolutions At Once,* issued in 1965. The civil rights movement, says the line, is part of a worldwide Communist revolutionary movement; it is Communist-inspired and Communist-dominated, and serves only Communist purposes.

The forces of the Radical Right energetically exploit the tensions and the street violence that discrimination has spawned. Forty-eight hours after the eruption of the 1965 Watts riots in Los Angeles, local Birch Society chapters in the area were mobilized, through a directive sent to all chapter leaders in the area, for an intensive propaganda drive to exploit white reaction to the tragedy.

The effort to utilize the white backlash and to whip it with a greater intensity, using the specter of Communism, has been plainly evident in other quarters.

Dr. Fred Schwarz, leader of the Christian Anti-Communism Crusade, suggested in a "Dear Friends" letter mailed within days of the Watts rioting that all expression of Negro grievances, "both legitimate and illegitimate," showed a sinister Communist influence, and that Negroes were chiefly responsible for ghetto conditions. "Behind the mob," he wrote, "there lurks the disciplined organization of the Communist Party ready to seize power once the destructive task is complete." (Oddly, Schwarz was referring here both to race riots and to collegiate panty-raids.)

Seven months after the Watts tragedy, on March 16, 1966, a relatively small disturbance in the same area provided Schwarz with an opportunity to exploit the race situation anew. He referred now to the Negro ghetto as a "security problem."

A 1965 letter sent to the Manion Forum's listeners warned that violence and racial strife were hurling the United States into chaos. The letter, nevertheless, dismissed the tragic murders of civil rights supporters in Selma, Alabama, such as Mrs. Viola Liuzzo and Rev. James Reeb, in almost casual fashion: the murders, it was conceded, were "sad, but they had no business being there, distant from their homes."

In fact, speaking himself about the "public expressions of sympathy, grief and anger" over the two murders, Manion commented that "no marchers mourned the death of a young man who was brutally killed on a New York subway." Manion's implication was that some sort of analogous relationship existed between the murders in Alabama and the murder in the subway, and he concluded that civil rights workers "seem to have the sole right to sympathy" —as though the New York victim had somehow been denied that right, or as though he believed that Mrs. Liuzzo and Reverend Reeb ought to have been denied it.

Among the leaders of the civil rights movement, the Rev. Martin Luther King, Jr., has been singled out for the greatest share of extremist venom. Alan Stang, in his book, *It's Very Simple,* the Birch Society's anti-civil rights handbook, accused Dr. King of being in effect "one of the country's most influential workers for Communism."

Billy James Hargis offers a propaganda package called *The Real 20th Century American Revolution,* in which he claims to reveal "the ugly truth about the near traitorous Martin Luther King."

Hargis protests against being called a racist, although the Christian Crusade has more than once recommended a book which argues that the Negro is innately inferior to

the white man—Carleton Putnam's *Race and Reason.*
Hargis, however, is a staunch segregationist and cites Scrip-
ture to support his view. "It is my conviction," he has
written, "that God ordained segregation. It is not because
I am against the Negro that I demand a maintenance of
racial segregation, it is because my mind must acknowledge
truth."

Hargis said he found the truth in Acts 17:26: "And hath
made of one blood all nations of men for to dwell on all
the face of the earth and hath determined the times before
appointed, and the *grounds of their habitation.*"

The emphasis was supplied by the Tulsa preacher to a
passage from the Bible which others might read as authority
and support for the concept of the brotherhood of all men
—"of one blood all nations of men. . . ."

But Hargis has long been on record against brotherhood. He once wrote:

No, my friends, brotherhood of all men is not a Christian concept; it is unchristian and even anti-christian.
Modernist destroyers of the faith are on thin ice when
they promote this false theory. Purpose of a Christian believer should not be to compromise the Christian
faith in the interests of so-called brotherhood, but to
bring men repentance of their sins and acceptance of
Jesus Christ as their personal Saviour. Those who would
water the Christian faith down into an all-inclusive
religion of togetherness would destroy the truth of our
Lord and Saviour.

It would appear that in the eyes of Hargis, the instruc-
tion that "Thou Shalt Love Thy Neighbor as Thyself" is
not part of the truth which Jesus imparted in his teachings.

Whatever the case, Hargis has maintained a steady
propaganda campaign on the subject of the civil rights
movement that generally follows the standard Radical
Rightist line, laced with doses of religious fundamentalism,

and has opposed civil rights legislation as opening doors "toward a totalitarian state."

The Washington-based Liberty Lobby has also fought fiercely against such legislation by the Congress. Of the Voting Rights Bill of 1965, *Liberty Letter* readers were told: "If the President's law is passed, the South will disappear from the civilized world."

Liberty Lobby also makes quantities of anti-civil rights literature available to its subscribers. Offerings during 1965 and 1966 included a "biography" of Alabama's George Wallace (possibly Liberty Lobby's "white hope" for 1968), a pamphlet called *Black Revolution is Red Revolution,* and copies of an abusive Congressional attack on civil rights marchers by Rep. William L. Dickinson (R., Ala.). In June, 1966, *Liberty Letter* offered a booklet for sale through its office called *Lawless Tyranny—An American Conspiracy Against We* [sic] *the People,* written by Joseph P. Kamp, a veteran extremist pamphleteer whose past writings have been filled with anti-Semitic innuendo. The Kamp booklet was offered as part of a "four-point plan to help defeat the Civil Rights Bill" (of 1966).

Dan Smoot also urged his readers and listeners to write their legislators. In June, 1966, he wrote:

> Bombard both houses of Congress with demands that *all* civil rights proposals be rejected this year. Urge all senators to refuse ratification of the UN Convention on the Elimination of All Forms of Racial Discrimination.

It is impossible to measure the extent to which the Radical Right's all-out propaganda warfare has helped create the white backlash. It certainly seems fair to say that its feverish outpourings both helped create the backlash and are helping to keep it alive.

It is a fact that organizations of the Radical Right have been marching shoulder to shoulder with the hard-core segregationists of the White Citizens' Councils in the war against the civil rights movement.

In exploiting racial tensions and violence, and the fears that flow from them, the Radical Right is, like the Communists, seeking to fill its coffers and its meeting halls from the fonts of human grief and human misery. And that is perhaps its greatest insult to the nation whose ideals it claims to revere.

CHAPTER FOUR

The Radical Right in Politics

The Radical Right has begun, in the middle years of the 1960s, to embark on an openly political program. The aim is to change the political thinking of Americans, and the ultimate target is political power.

Two approaches are now being employed in the effort —and these are contradictory and competing tactics, a fact which has introduced some disagreement in the ranks, though certainly only a tactical disagreement. Some Rightist leaders favor the infiltration of a major political party with the aim of capturing it; others propose a Far Right Wing "third party" as the movement's only hope.

During the Presidential election of 1964, the legions of America's Radical Right became some of the more active campaign workers, misusing the Republican Party's national effort as a vehicle for their own special purposes of propaganda and recruitment. The most obvious immediate benefactor was The John Birch Society, whose members attached themselves to the legitimate campaign and used it for their own ideological purposes.

"As a partisan Republican," said Sen. Thruston Morton of Kentucky, a former Republican National Chairman and a GOP moderate, "I am concerned by the fact that The John Birch Society has picked my party . . . as a vehicle to promulgate its monolithic philosophy."

But the infiltration of a major political party is not the project of just one organization, nor is it the only road to political power now under consideration. The extremist camps have been split—tactically—on the question of which political road to take.

Capture the GOP, or organize a third party?

"The liberals of both the Democrat and Republican Parties," says Christian Crusade leader Billy James Hargis, "are the instruments of Satan to destroy the former great principles of these two political parties . . ." To this view most of the leaders of the Radical Right subscribe. Their opinions divide as to whether at least one of the traditional parties can be "saved" by determined Rightist infiltration or whether the only road to political power is through a new party of their own, predicated on the notion that a majority of Americans can be persuaded that the country needs to be saved and that the job can be done by the application of Radical Right formulas.

The capture of the Republican Party by the Radical Right has been a professed aim of Liberty Lobby, one of the most significant of newly ascendant extremist groups, and has been a thinly veiled objective of The John Birch Society's new political cadre. The third-party road has been championed primarily by Kent Courtney, head of the Conservative Society of America, who has pressed for that policy almost continually for the past eight years.

The Third Party Movement

Courtney, a Bircher and an avid segregationist with headquarters in New Orleans, first exposed his "third-party" plan in 1959. As one of the chief non-Republican backers of Senator Goldwater at the 1960 GOP convention (he sponsored a Goldwater rally in Chicago which was addressed by Robert Welch), Courtney was disenchanted with the Republicans, including Goldwater, after they chose Nixon as their candidate. Courtney immediately retreated to the separatist camp, and at a third-party rally he staged in 1961, described Goldwater as a compromiser "tainted by socialism." This coolness toward the Arizona Senator continued (Courtney's headquarters issued a pamphlet called, *Is Goldwater Really a Conservative?*) until Senator Goldwater announced early in 1964 that he would actively seek the nomination. Once again Courtney became an ardent Goldwater backer.

The third-party talk began again in late April, 1965, when Courtney convened a "Congress of Conservatives" in Chicago, a mammoth three-day convention of Radical Rightists and segregationists, which was to hear from such speakers as the Birchers' Robert Welch, Let Freedom Ring's William Douglass, segregationist Lester Maddox of Georgia, Dr. Medford Evans (whose name appears on mastheads of both the White Citizens' Councils and Welch's *American Opinion*), Willis E. Stone, head of the Liberty Amendment movement, and chairman Courtney himself.

Courtney strongly urged the formation of a new party, suggesting that this had been the convention's purpose.

Harry T. Everingham, director of a small Far Right coalition called "We, the People!," dissented. Leading Republicans had assured him, Everingham declared, that the GOP had "not been taken over by the socialist liberals" but was still under Goldwaterite control, and was the only conservative hope for victory in the 1966 Congressional elections. He added, however, that there would be a new Right Wing party "after the minds of people can be fertilized."

Robert Welch told those assembled that his presence was not to be interpreted as either approval or disapproval of the third-party idea by The John Birch Society.

Lester Maddox declared his support for Alabama's governor, George Wallace, for President in 1968—and there were cheers from the audience. (Kent Courtney later told Illinois Rightists that third-party advocates had been ready to go with Wallace in 1964, had Goldwater failed to win the GOP nomination.)

Courtney stated that no new party was to emerge from the Chicago "congress," but that plans for its formation would be worked out by a five-man committee just appointed, serving under the chairmanship of Medford Evans.

Under Courtney's appointed leaders, a 39-member committee was established to set up the grass-roots operation in various states. The "third party" was to be molded under a platform of pure Radical Right appeal. It was to include planks urging United States withdrawal from the United Nations, the breaking of diplomatic relations with all "Communist" countries, the liberation of Cuba and Red China, an end to all civil rights legislation, the establishment of more restrictive immigration quotas, and repeal of the income tax.

By the time of Courtney's "congress," Rightist parties (not necessarily Radical or necessarily allied with the New Orleans leader) were already functioning in New York, New Jersey, Texas, Virginia, Louisiana, Washington, Kansas, and Iowa.

Four months later, on September 25, 1965, Right Wingers in Michigan formed the American Party, whose founding convention was addressed by Courtney. In December, the American Party unanimously passed a resolution calling upon Michigan to secede from the United States.

Illinois Rightists got rolling on October 2, with a meeting at which Courtney again was the speaker.

Those in Georgia held a "new party" conference on October 16, and those in Pennsylvania on December 11. From the Georgia meeting emerged the "American Party" —its name and its Courtney affiliations similar to those of Michigan, and its chaplain the Rev. George Birch, father of John Birch.

Dr. William Douglass, director of Let Freedom Ring, had meanwhile announced the formation of a Rightist party in Florida.

Some of the older "third parties" began to offer their podiums to extremist speakers who have appeared on the scene in more recent years. Thus, in January, 1966, the Constitution Party of Texas held a party meeting and heard addresses by two outspoken anti-Semites—broadcaster Richard Cotten and Ned Touchstone, editor of *The Councilor*, the Louisiana White Citizens' Council organ published in Shreveport.

In Missouri, the American Conservative Party listed the same address as the local Workers for Wallace group. The American Conservative Party was headed by Floyd G. Kitchen, a member of the national board of advisors of Courtney's Conservative Society of America. Kitchen was also president of the St. Louis Property Owners Association, which sponsored a local appearance of J. B. Stoner, vice chairman of the racist, anti-Semitic National States Rights Party and a onetime Ku Klux Klan organizer. The representative of Kitchen's party at Courtney's Chicago "congress" was James Kernodle, a former John Birch Society section leader who once introduced Robert DePugh, leader of the armed, para-military Minutemen to a local Rightist audience.

Robert DePugh himself held his own third-party convention in Kansas City, on July 4, 1966. DePugh told a St. Louis *Post-Dispatch* reporter that the Minutemen were working to form a united membership drawn from about 30 small but militant organizations of the extreme Right, that it would be called the Patriotic Party, and that its members would also try to infiltrate the two major parties.

In point of fact, the Patriotic Party that emerged appeared to be a poorly disguised political arm for the Minutemen, those who train and drill with weapons in secret, organized in bands supposedly for future anti-Communist guerrilla warfare. This program of activity stems from their claimed conviction that the United States is already largely in the hands of the Reds and that the completion of the takeover will occur in the next few years.

Regional meetings of the Patriotic Party were held early in September, 1966, in several cities scattered across the country, and were addressed, via telephone, by DePugh and by Kenneth Goff, a former lieutenant of Gerald Smith, long-time anti-Semitic rabble-rouser. Goff is a notorious anti-Semite in his own right. Among others who addressed the Patriotic Party gatherings were John Martino, listed a few years ago as a speaker available through The John Birch Society's lecture bureau, and anti-Semite Richard Cotten.

By the fall of 1966, the Patriotic Party had spawned units in a few widely scattered states—Texas, California, Washington, Oklahoma, Arizona and Connecticut—and had drawn to its banners a small but zealous following of the far-out Right. DePugh claimed followers in 41 states.

In a sense, the Patriotic Party was the visible peak of a submerged and clandestine Radical Right iceberg—the Minutemen—who were beginning to receive increasing attention from law enforcement authorities. DePugh himself has had several run-ins with the law. In the fall of 1966, during his trial on charges of violating the Federal Firearms Act, a member of the Minutemen testified that the band had discussed plans to assassinate Sen. William Fulbright, Chairman of the Senate Foreign Relations Committee, and a scheme to put cyanide gas in the air-conditioning ducts at the UN headquarters building in New York.

On November 14, 1966, DePugh was convicted of conspiracy and of possession of automatic weapons or silencers without registering them, and of not paying a federal transfer tax on them. On January 17, 1967, he was sentenced to four years in federal prison, to be followed by five years on probation. Troy Houghton, West Coast coordinator of the Minutemen, was sentenced to three years in prison, and

Walter P. Peyson, an aide to DePugh, received two years in jail and three on probation. U. S. Judge Elmo Hunter, who pronounced the sentences, ordered that during the probationary periods, the convicted Minutemen could not belong to any organization using weapons illegally. If they joined any military type of organization, they were to tell their probation officer about it and provide him with the names of the organization's officers.

After the sentencing, DePugh was quoted as saying that a "liberal-Communist-socialist" conspiracy controls the United States Government and that this had led to "the unfair and unconstitutional investigative procedures that brought this to court."

A few days later, he resigned as national coordinator of the Minutemen. DePugh said the identity of the leader or leaders who would replace him would be kept secret. He said the organization would operate under a new secret code system by which its members would be identified to each other.

At the end of January, 1967, DePugh pleaded *nolo contendere* on a separate charge—that he violated another Federal law by transporting a revolver from Iowa to Kansas City while under indictment for another offense. The court told him his plea of *nolo contendere*—in which the defendant does not admit the charge but does not present his case in defense—would be treated as a plea of guilty and that there would be no appeal. DePugh was sentenced to a year in prison—the sentence not to begin until his appeal on the other conviction was decided. The court said that whenever a decision was made on the appeal, it would have no effect on the one-year sentence.

Equally startling was a roundup of 20 alleged Minutemen in New York's Borough of Queens on charges that they were planning to bomb three camps in upstate New York, which they reportedly believed were gathering places for Leftist elements and pacifist sympathizers.

In his 1966 book, *Blueprint for Victory*, DePugh spelled out the way he viewed the role of political parties in the struggle:

(1) Political action *alone* will not suffice.
(2) A new political party cannot win by *conventional means.*
(3) A new party can win if it serves its proper function as the political arm of a complete patriotic resistance movement.

The Patriotic Party, soon after it was formed, began attracting extremists and anti-Semites to its ranks and emerged as a haven for those on the Right who had become impatient with the less flamboyant programs of other groups who claim they are working to save the country.

The "Third Party" Rationale

The whole rationale for a new party was expressed by Kent Courtney in a pamphlet published shortly after the 1964 Presidential election and entitled *Liberal Takeover of GOP Will Trigger New Party*. In it, the energetic third-party theorist wrote that moderate Republicans had designed a "semisecret plan" for party control. He went on to quote Barry Goldwater's promise to "continue to be a working member of the Republican Party—not trying to dictate anything, just putting my shoulder to the wheel."

"Thus," commented Courtney, "did Goldwater 'telegraph' to his 27 million supporters that he did not intend to fight for Conservative principles . . ." And there was a tone in Courtney's words suggesting: I once told you so, during my vacillations in and out of the Goldwater camp.

Courtney was *out* again—once more seeking to lead the major attempt to form a new political party. An Alaskan who resigned from the GOP to work for the new party wrote to him:

"You're trying to do the impossible, but I'll help you do it."

The way in which it was to be done, as Courtney explained it to a meeting of the Illinois party group:

"If we could win one seat from each of the fifty states, we couldn't control Congress, but we could prevent pro-socialistic and Communistic legislation from passing."

He said that conservatives would be a "polarizing" agent in Congress, pulling Rightists from both traditional sides of the aisle.

Late in 1965, Courtney made a brief attempt to polarize sentiments in New York City's mayoralty election. He sent a letter to about one thousand New Yorkers urging them to vote for William F. Buckley, Jr., candidate of New York's Conservative Party (not a Courtney affiliate). The letter referred to GOP candidate John V. Lindsay as "pro-Communist." Others on the Courtney letterhead were Medford Evans and E. Merrill Root of *American Opinion,* and Frank Ranuzzi, Radical Rightist bookstore operator (Poor Richard's Book Shop, now in Hamilton, Mont.) who had a record of peddling anti-Semitic literature.

William Buckley himself, repudiating the letter, termed it "utterly and totally irresponsible . . . straight Birchite vocabulary."

While Kent Courtney agitated and recruited at the grass roots for his "third party," one man appeared to have begun seriously considering himself an appropriate Presidential candidate of such a movement. This was Alabama's George Wallace, who made a good showing in several Northern Democratic primaries in 1964—43% of the vote in Maryland, 34% in Wisconsin, and 30% in Indiana. In mid-1966 stumping, Wallace, the arch foe of integration, issued barbed attacks on the Democratic and Republican parties alike, convinced perhaps that the white backlash and his own ultra-conservative and pro-segregationist views could be a boon to his serious 1968 candidacy.

At the same time, however, there was other Right Wing agitation at the grass roots—with different goals and different appeals. Capture the Republican Party at the precinct level, cried others on the Far Right, and then work toward greater political influence and ultimate political power within the traditional two-party system. The advocates of this approach—infiltration and precinct-level work toward party control—are probably more numerous and probably more practical than the advocates of "new" and "third" parties.

And they have plans.

Capturing the GOP

In addition to the political activities recommended to its members by The John Birch Society, those of still another Radical Right organization are of major importance in the plan to infiltrate and gain control of the Republican Party.

That organization is Liberty Lobby, the fast-growing Washington political action and pressure group which maintains friendly relations with some ultra-conservative members of Congress, generates barrages of mail on legislative issues of major concern to the Far Right, and publishes the widely circulated *Liberty Letter*.

As a leading organization of the American Radical Right, Liberty Lobby places little faith in the potentials of a third party, and adheres firmly to the idea of operating within the two-party system. Its views were set forth just after the 1964 election in its "inside" publication, *Liberty Lowdown*, which reaches a more limited and perhaps more politically sophisticated readership:

> The Goldwater defeat of November 3 was just what the left-wingers in the GOP wanted and worked for. Hand in hand with the Communist Party . . . they succeeded in misleading the voters. Now, backed by Wall Street billions, the press and all the artifices of the Conspira-

tors they are closing in for what they hope will be the kill. If they succeed in wresting control of the Republican Party from Conservatives . . . never again will there be a chance to rescue Freedom and Constitutional Government from the abyss.

Liberty Lobby has declared that a third party, unless it can itself achieve ruling power, only provides a focal point for splinter ideas (as with the Populists) or a balance-of-power mechanism in order to swing close elections to "lesser of two evils" between the major parties. The leaders of Liberty Lobby, always realistic, have seen no chance of a third party victory, nor on the other hand have they regarded their cause as a splinter movement. Obviously, one of the major parties must be made palatable for radicals of the Right—from within.

These leaders have proposed a "party within a party" approach—an infiltration technique to be put to work "in every state where control of the GOP is not already in conservative hands." The plan was published early in 1965 as *The Conservative Victory Plan*—a blueprint for grassroots political activity aimed at control of precinct and state party organizations through infiltration by a dedicated and self-styled conservative minority.

In basic contradiction to the professed views and methods of The John Birch Society, Liberty Lobby's planner declared that "education is not the key any longer." In a colorful 32-page brochure entitled *Looking Forward* (an expanded version of the original *Conservative Victory Plan*) published late in 1965, Liberty Lobby planners wrote that the only conceivable shape of Right Wing victory is political.

"How much is annually spent by Conservatives in a wide range of non-political activity is difficult to estimate," they wrote, "but it is surely more than ten million dollars." They added:

"These non-political activities have some value to the

overall Conservative impact upon the Country but their value is less and less proportionally as the opportunity for direct political action grows."

Liberty Lobby's executive director, W. B. Hicks, called upon "all Conservatives" to consolidate their control of local Republican precinct organizations and expand into those areas not yet controlled. Hicks saw 250,000 dedicated workers as sufficient "to control the politics of the country."

Through its large mailings, Liberty Lobby has sought to reach deep into the GOP rank and file to propagate its ideas and recruit a cadre. The extent of this reach grew considerably greater when the Republican National Committee's mailing list was sold to Liberty Lobby after the 1964 election. The sale was the idea (for raising funds) of Frank Kovac, a holdover in the GOP who had been finance chairman of Citizens for Goldwater and Miller.

To carry out its political blueprint, Liberty Lobby has the services of the United Republicans of America, which has office space in the same Washington building. URA appeared at first to be the activity of one man, D. Bruce Evans, but it soon became clear that it was the political action arm of Liberty Lobby and perhaps the nucleus of the actual "party-within-a-party" that aims at taking over the GOP.

Another long-time Rightist voice recently launched his own program for capturing the Republican Party—a long-range plan to develop a Far Right "youth" movement. He is H. L. Hunt, the Texas oil billionaire, who has stated that "immediate planning for the formation of a workable Republican Party is imperative."

Hunt's project was the formation of a Public Service Education Institute, actually designed to promote promising young political hopefuls and candidates in deliberate secrecy.

According to Hunt, as quoted in *The New York Times* in December, 1964, the institute was to recruit 50 state directors and a supervisor in each Congressional district to seek out and promote potential candidates without the subjects' knowledge.

The PLAN (Hunt capitalized it) was rationalized on one of the oil man's radio broadcasts in this way:

> History has proved the haphazard form of selecting and preparing candidates for elective offices is fatal, with ill-equipped officials compounding the error by appointing other unqualified individuals to offices upon which our nation's independence must rely. The PLAN is arranged to carry forward, quietly and unofficially, the ideals of providing trained "statesmen" to guide our nation.

The PLAN itself suggests:

> PROSPECTS are needed, age 20 to 60 years. If a man is more than 26 years of age, he should be married and preferably the father of one to 4 children . . . He should be ambitious to attain higher office . . . The hobbies of a PROSPECT are important . . . With the prevalent fear of lung cancer, it will be slightly better if the PROSPECT does not smoke . . . He should be popular and a good mixer . . . The PROSPECT should have a pleasing name, easy to pronounce and spell, and one suggesting statesmanship and Americanism, unless it is a name popular to nationalities and races among the electorate in his particular area.

The appearance of a Hunt-sponsored organization called Youth Freedom Speakers suggests that the oil man's PLAN, perhaps in modified form, is already in operation. The Youth Freedom Speakers group has been sponsoring public speeches by clean-cut, wholesome, and bright young people who, presumably, reflect viewpoints acceptable to Hunt.

Hunt's effort to develop future political candidates is not the only long-range political project under way on the Radical Right. During 1966, formation of The 1976 Committee was announced. This group was headed by William

J. Grede, a Milwaukee industrialist who is a member of the National Council of The John Birch Society and chairman of its Executive Committee. Grede stated that half the 30 founding members of The 1976 Committee were Birchers, but to what extent the new group was an arm or front of the Society was not immediately clear.

There was no question, however, that it was clearly political in concept and in purpose. Formed on April 30, 1966, the group in November of the same year announced that it had "launched a 10-year crusade to assure a conservative executive branch of the Federal Government." The drive was touched off by the mailing to "conservatives throughout the U.S." of 385,000 copies of a 16-page booklet explaining The 1976 Committee's goals.

The booklet, announcing the ten-year effort "to restore the American Republic," painted a dark picture of "tremendously powerful and solidly entrenched forces at work, right here on American soil, which are determined to abolish our nation's independence." The committee said those forces "are now visibly striving to make this once great country simply a group of provinces under a one-world socialist government." And it added, "at their present rate of progress . . . they will have accomplished their aims completely in 1976."

In order "to stop this gradual surrender of American sovereignty into the grasp of a cruel worldwide tyranny," The 1976 Committee declared, it, too, had taken 1976 as its "target date." And it vowed to stop "this whole nightmare of insanity and subversion"—by "ten years of supreme sacrifice and effort"—and dissolve itself on July 4, 1976, the 200th anniversary of American independence.

The first step, the Committee declared, was "to create massive support for Ezra Taft Benson"—Secretary of Agriculture in the Eisenhower cabinet—for President of the United States in the 1968 election, and for Republican Sen. Strom Thurmond of South Carolina for Vice-President. The 1976 Committee said it would set up affiliated

State and Local 1976 Clubs, or Supporters of the 1976 Committee.

The 16-page booklet proposed that the effort for Benson and Thurmond "be directed, by Conservative Democrats and Conservative Republicans alike, at making these two men the candidates of *both parties*" and admitted that this was "an unusual course." It said this would help replace "bi-partisan treason" with "bi-partisan patriotism" but added that "we are not by any means suggesting the abandonment or weakening of the two-party system." All it sought to do, the group said, was "to lift a political movement which is designed to meet a particular crisis, and to be temporary rather than permanent, into the level of a national patriotic crusade."

The booklet contained a reading list of standard Far Right books and pamphlets and gave places where the materials could be purchased, including the Birch Society's headquarters and the Society's network of American Opinion bookstores.

Whether The 1976 Committee represents a venture by The John Birch Society into the political arena of the next decade or not, the Society, always denying its political character, already has a political thrust of its own—as will be seen later. It is worth remembering that, as one former Society coordinator put it in the flush of the 1964 political campaign, the Birch organization aims to control American political thinking by 1968. Whether, in fact, 1968—or 1972 and 1976—will see the climax of the Radical Right challenge to America is a question for history.

The dangers of infiltration into the political party structure, however, are clear in the light of events already transpiring.

The Rat Finks

What can happen to an established political organization when infiltrated by mobilized segments of the Radical

Right was vividly demonstrated in the case of the "Rat Finks"—a so-called conservative faction that bloomed in the New Jersey Young Republican organization. Dissension and turmoil were the fruits of its activity, and political embarrassment the price paid by the party as a result of the infiltration.

Some Rat Finks, of a membership estimated at several hundred, were accused of singing (and distributing song-sheets for) a number of anti-Semitic and racist songs at the YR state convention at Wildwood in May, 1965, and at the national convention in Miami in June. One, mimeographed and spread among the crowds attending the conventions, asked, "Where has all the welfare gone?"— and provided the answer, "Gone to the niggers." Another song went as follows (to the tune of *Jingle Bells*):

> Riding through the Reich
> In my Mercedes-Benz,
> Shooting every kike,
> Saving all my friends.
> Rat-tat-tat
> Rat-tat-tat
> Mow the bastards down,
> Oh, what fun it is to have
> The Nazis back in town.

GOP State Senator Nelson Stamler made public the accusations against the Rat Finks on the basis of an eye-witness account by a young lady YR from Idaho who had been present at the Wildwood convention. He described the faction as "a group of extreme right-wing bigots who would destroy the party."

The case produced newspaper headlines across the country, charges and countercharges, and a series of hearings, trials, and investigations by state, local, and national YR units. It also produced considerable concern in the highest councils of the senior Republican Party, both in New Jersey and in Washington, D.C. The proceedings dragged on for several months.

During 1966, the national executive committee of the Young Republicans ruled that Rat Fink members must either quit the faction or get out of the YR organization. The purge was also broadened to exclude from the New Jersey chapter all members of The John Birch Society or any other factional group. The leader of the Rat Finks was absolved of charges of bigotry and anti-Semitism, but was forced to resign as YR national vice-chairman for the New Jersey, New York, Pennsylvania and Delaware area.

Several county units in New Jersey were suspended and later took court action to gain readmission to the YR family. The YR state committee later reinstated these units in a compromise stipulating that they behave. But hopes that these actions would ease the Rat Fink problem were soon dashed and the small Rat Fink minority continued to be troublesome in New Jersey.

Early in 1967, the state senior GOP took complete control of the New Jersey YR organization. Control was vested in an eight-member board of "trustees" composed of leading Republicans. Almost no action could be taken by the YRs—meetings and elections were included—without the approval of the senior board, who were also to control the election of delegates to national and regional YR conventions. The senior group could also repudiate any statements by the YRs too far out of line with party policies. Any county chapters not cooperating in housecleaning efforts could have their charters revoked and assigned to friendly groups.

It became clear, however, that the propagandists and activists of the outer rightist fringes had begun to move into the openly political arena.

Such activity cannot be written off as a threat in a country passing through a profound racial crisis at home and difficult times overseas—precisely the conditions that activists, whether of the Communist Left or the Radical Right, seek to exploit for their own ends. In the meantime, all the resources of radio propaganda, the press,

57

electronic recording, and all the techniques of infiltration and membership recruitment have been mobilized for the Radical Right's thrust toward political influence and power.

The 1966 Elections

Whatever the long-range plans of the Radical Right may be for ultimate political influence and power, the movement is finding cold comfort at the polls—at least for the present.

Whether running under third-party banners or under the standards of the two major parties, Radical Rightist candidates in the 1966 elections received short shrift from the voters, as they had in 1962 and 1964. Here and there, a few Birchers or a few non-Birch Radical Rightists managed to slip onto the ballots in various states, but few, if any, were victorious.

A handful of Birchers (see Chapter 11) won seats in state legislatures—two in California, two in Wisconsin, one in Florida, one in Utah, and another in Alaska.

The ultra-segregationist segment of the Radical Right could, perhaps, take some satisfaction from the victory of Mrs. Lurleen Wallace in the race for Governor of Alabama, the more so because it sees her husband as a 1968 Presidential hopeful. The segregationists might also take comfort from the surprising showing and subsequent election of their candidate, Lester Maddox, in the Georgia gubernatorial campaign, and from the election to Congress of John R. Rarick, a leader of the Louisana White Citizens' Councils.

Nevertheless, such brassy voices of segregation and white backlash as Jim Johnson and George Mahoney went down to defeat in their bids for the governors' chairs in Arkansas and Maryland respectively.

Sheriff Jim Clark of Dallas County, Alabama, a symbol of segregation and resistance to Negro rights at Selma and a speaker for the Birch Society lecture bureau, lost his post in the Democratic primary. His write-in bid in November also failed.

Thousands of elective public offices were contested in 1966, and many candidates of genuinely conservative outlook were elected, but save for the handful of Birchers, the American people so far do not appear to place their trust in exponents of the Radical Rightist political viewpoint.

CHAPTER FIVE

The Hazy Borderlines

The Radical Right forms only a segment of the American Right Wing movement of the 1960s. Alongside, but nearer the political center where the voices of reason are heard and where the process of compromise takes place, is that sector of the American Right which can truly be called "conservative."

While it is not always easy to place Rightists in one category or the other, there are basic differences between the two that are not mere matters of semantic quibbling. The hallmark of the Radical Right viewpoint is the firm belief that the United States has been for many years in the grip of a deep-seated and powerful internal Communist conspiracy, which has penetrated all aspects of American life, pervading the labor movement, the clergy, the business world, the media of mass communication, and the academic world at the university level.

Extreme conservatives oppose many of the same programs opposed by the Radical Right. But these conservatives blame such trends in American policy on stupidity, blindness, and bungling by liberals and moderates—whom they tend to lump together as the so-called "Liberal Establishment"—rather than on an internal Communist conspiracy entrenched in Washington and throughout American society.

Some conservatives view the Radical Right's insistence on the conspiracy theory as "paranoid and unpatriotic drivel"—which is how William F. Buckley, Jr., perhaps conservatism's most articulate spokesman, described the propaganda themes of The John Birch Society.

The difference in viewpoint between the Radical Right and these conservatives was epitomized, in October, 1965, by a series of articles by Buckley and his editorial colleagues on *National Review* magazine. They concluded, in an in-depth examination, that members of the Birch Society were not merely misguided conservatives following a radical leader—Robert Welch—but that in fact they appeared to believe Welch's conspiracy theories and to accept what Buckley called Welch's "surrealisms."

Two months after the *National Review* articles, Buckley indicated in an interview in the Baltimore *Evening Sun* that it might be desirable (though impossible, he thought) to purge certain radicals of the Right from the conservative side. He specifically named Willis E. Stone's Liberty Amendment Committee and the para-military Minutemen.

The Radical Rightists have been noticeably shocked and angered by the Buckley attacks. "His declaration of war on the Birch Society will ruin him," said Billy James Hargis. Buckley was "malinformed and misinformed," said Kent Courtney. At Hargis's Christian Crusade convention in 1966, Birch Society National Council member Tom Anderson declared Buckley to be "not only a menace to Robert Welch, but to the English language" (his words, said Anderson, showed egomania and jealousy). A large banner spread across a wall in the convention's literature room read:

"Et tu, Buckley?"

The implication of betrayal was not intended as a joke. And yet there were signs that the major share of the bitterness was to be found among only a few Radical Rightist leaders, extending but little to the rank and file, and that it had not destroyed the possibility of collaboration between some extreme conservatives and those of the more radical fringe.

Buckley himself has failed to undertake anything like a thorough and sustained effort to rid the American Right of its extremist radicals. While indicating that it might have been desirable to do so, he has not put his own considerable intellectual and leadership attributes to the task.

A full year after the *National Review* articles, there still existed, more noticeably than ever, a patchwork of hazy borderlines in some areas of Rightist activity—an ideological "blur" where extreme conservatives all too often could, and did, mingle in common causes with Radical Rightists because the basic philosophical differences did not matter to those involved, or were not clearly recognized to begin with. Originally, that had been the situation with Buckley; it is no longer.

Take the case of retired Admiral Ben Moreell, chairman of Americans for Constitutional Action (ACA), an ultra-conservative group which offers both moral and financial support to political candidates of firm and established conservative principles. In 1966, Admiral Moreell accepted a vice-chairmanship of The 1976 Committee, half of whose members were identified with The John Birch Society. Another vice-chairman was Loyd Wright, also a leader in ACA and one of the nation's leading conservatives.

Or take the case of Maj. Gen. Thomas A. Lane, also of ACA, and a prominent speaker on the conservative circuit. In June, 1966, he shared a platform with Buckley's brother-in-law, L. Brent Bozell, and ultra-conservative author Phyllis Schlafly. But in May, 1965, Lane had also addressed the Birch Society's "American Opinion Forum" in Philadelphia, an event listed in the Society's monthly *Bulletin*. (For her part, Mrs. Schlafly had lent her name to radicals of Liberty Lobby, as chief speaker at their 1965 dinner.)

General Lane's views have also seemed, to some observers, to contradict the conservative image. He once called U Thant, the UN's Secretary-General, "an agent of the Soviet Union in exacting concessions from the United States."

Lane on civil rights: ". . . In an emotional fervor to win white citizen accommodation to Negro demands, national leaders mouthed a fictitious history of Negro oppression and discrimination in the United States which was hardly distinguishable from the Communist line."

Lane on the Birch Society: "The John Birch Society is dedicated to fighting Communism and its dupes, adherents, and associates. It stands for long-honored American principles . . ."

The extreme conservative Young Americans for Freedom —YAF—have worn the Buckley image since their formation at his Connecticut home back in 1960. Their 1966 New England conference, however, offered a platform to E. Merrill Root, one of the editors of Robert Welch's *American Opinion* magazine.

The ideological blur can also be seen in the fact that YAF's Western Director, Ted Loeffler, is an important executive in Constructive Action, Inc., which distributes such Radical Rightist tomes as Stormer's *None Dare Call It Treason* and Alan Stang's Birchite interpretation of the civil rights movement—both saturated with the conspiracy theories typical of Radical Right thinking.

E. Merrill Root and Prof. Hans Sennholz, another of Welch's stable of writers for *American Opinion,* sit on a committee of "textbook evaluators" for America's Future, Inc., an extreme conservative organization in New Rochelle, New York, which provides what it calls "documented information regarding the textbooks now in use in the high schools of the nation." The fact that evaluators Root and Sennholz have for some time been identified with Welch's ideological family does not appear to have disqualified them in the eyes of America's Future, Inc.

The flabby thinking which makes possible collaboration

by some extreme conservatives with Radical Right organizations and leaders is reminiscent of dalliances by some liberals with Radicals of the Far Left in bygone years. But the liberals carried out a thorough housecleaning during the late 1940s and 1950s—the kind of housecleaning that is long overdue on the American Right.

National Review editor Frank S. Meyer has written that "the John Birch Society is rapidly losing whatever it had in common with patriotism or conservatism." And yet a great many conservatives in the United States apparently have not yet awakened to that fact.

Anti-Semitism

Other hazy borderlines lie between the Radical Right and those to its right—the peddlers of overt or disguised anti-Semitism.

Some Radical Right organizations have had a chronic problem of anti-Semitism in their midst—a problem stemming from a lack of alertness or a lack of concern. Organizations such as Liberty Lobby do not consider the presence of anti-Semites in their midst to be a problem at all. If they do not seek, they at least appear to welcome the support of known Jew-haters.

Liberty Lobby's chairman, Col. Curtis B. Dall, testifying against President Kennedy's trade-expansion bill in August, 1962, declared: "The real center and heart of this international cabal shows its hand; namely, the Political Zionist Planners for Absolute Rule, via One World Government."

In addition to Dall, Liberty Lobby's Board of Policy, shortly after the organization began its swift rise as an influence both on the Radical Right and in extremist political circles, included such anti-Semites as Richard Cotten, Joseph Kamp, Ned Touchstone, and Kenneth Goff.

The real organizer behind Liberty Lobby has been Willis Carto, until 1960 identified with *RIGHT,* an anti-Jewish newsletter published in the San Francisco Bay area by an organization called Liberty and Property. Carto's associate in Liberty and Property, Bruce Holman, in 1966 became chairman of the board of a re-organized *American Mercury* magazine, whose masthead showed a distinct Liberty Lobby influence. Listed as contributing editors were such Liberty Lobby personalities as Dall, Kamp, Touchstone, and Goff. Along with Goff, another anti-Semite—W. Henry MacFarland, Jr.—was added to the *Mercury's* masthead in its Winter, 1966, issue. The back cover of that issue carried an advertisement for *Money Made Mysterious,* an anti-Semitic pamphlet assembled from articles which had appeared in *American Mercury* in the late 1950s, when it was heavily flavored with blatant anti-Semitism.

The "new" *Mercury* which made its appearance on the scene in June, 1966, included a joint subscription arrangement with another publication—The *Washington Observer Newsletter,* published twice monthly since 1965 from a Washington post office box and edited by someone called Lee Roberts. Roberts had been commentator for a radio program sponsored by Liberty Lobby in the early 1960s, but no longer on the air. *Washington Observer Newsletter,* like the magazine, *American Mercury,* showed clear signs of anti-Semitic bias in several of its 1966 issues.

And if further evidence were needed, the *Mercury* announced in June, 1966, that it had taken over subscriptions to *Western Destiny,* a defunct racist publication and that it had "therefore become heir to *Northern World, Folk* and *RIGHT,* publications to which *WD* was successor." *Northern World* and *Folk* were racist periodicals; *RIGHT,* as has been noted, was racist and anti-Jewish, and served as a clearing-house for news about anti-Semitic groups.

Other organizations on the Radical Right have for years tolerated anti-Semites in the ranks and on their speakers' platforms. One of these is the Congress of Freedom, an older group with headquarters in Omaha. The 1966 annual meeting of COF, held at Shreveport, La., was addressed by such anti-Semites as Ned Touchstone, Richard Cotten, retired Admiral John G. Crommelin of Alabama, and Mrs. Opal Tanner White, a longtime associate of bigot Gerald Smith.

The blur between political extremism and the overt hate fringe runs along the nether borders of the Radical Right. At the 1965 convention of the Hargis Christian Crusade, former Maj. Gen. Edwin A. Walker, in speaking of the man who killed Lee Harvey Oswald, President Kennedy's assassin, urged his listeners not to forget "that Ruby's name was Rubenstein, and they can't change that no matter how often they refer to him as Ruby."

Hargis himself has recommended to his followers that they listen to the radio broadcasts of anti-Semite Richard Cotten.

And so it goes—a blindness with respect to bigotry and a tendency to attract anti-Semites to their causes, which seem to characterize much of the Radical Right today. The trouble, of course, has its roots in the acceptance of a conspiracy theory of history, with its different meanings for different people. When Americans are convinced that their government and their destinies are under the control of Communists, it is not a far stretch of gullibility to see still other identities in the camps of the plotters. For some of the listeners to the propaganda voices of the Radical Right, the door to religious hatred is easily opened. All too often the leaders of extremist organizations of the Right have failed to notice, or to consider as serious, the fact that the door is there.

CHAPTER SIX

Today
and Tomorrow

The Radical Right of the 1960s has firmly entrenched itself on the American scene, and has made its plans for the coming political and ideological battles. The gains of the 1964 Presidential year have been, for the most part, solidified. They were not undone in the 1966 elections. The overgrowth of this period has been weeded and cleared, some of the branches pruned for further development in the future. Most of the larger Far Rightist organizations made the transition to the less hectic post-election period smoothly, and by the beginning of 1967 were launching new projects to extend their thrust.

At the height of the 1964-65 excitement in the movement, several of its leading organizations were suddenly presented with a nettling problem: the loss of their tax exemptions as religious or educational institutions. The Internal Revenue Service revoked the tax-exempt status of H.L. Hunt's Life Line Foundation and Circuit Riders, Inc., and notified Billy James Hargis that similar action was contemplated against the Christian Crusade because "a substantial part of your operation is directed at the accomplishment of political objectives." The IRS finalized its action against Hargis in October, 1966.

The tax-exempt status allows a contributor to deduct funds from his income tax return that he donated to religious or educational organizations—and such status is often a major factor in group fund-raising efforts. Organizations that receive considerable income from large contributors are more dependent on tax-deductibility than are groups relying upon small contributors, who send in dollar bills, fives and tens. Many Radical Right groups, however, are sustained by repeated small contributions from the same individual, and this sometimes adds up to a tidy total at the end of a year, so that even these organizations can be benefitted by tax-deductibility.

Despite such problems, the Radical Right continues to operate with durable vigor—in the big cities and the suburbs, and in towns and hamlets of rural America as well. It is well financed and well staffed for its huge radio, publishing, and recruitment endeavors.

The movement is a permanent fixture on the American political scene—at least for the foreseeable future. And as 1967 began, its leading organizations were at work with a broad variety of plans and activities aimed at 1968 and beyond.

• Liberty Lobby, already established as one of the fastest growing of such organizations, was in the midst of a major fund-raising drive for its openly political activities. It sought to boost the operating budget—more than $400,000 in 1966—for larger lobbying efforts on Capitol Hill, for efforts to generate mail barrages from its followers on legislation pending in Congress, and for long-range efforts to capture the Republican Party from within.

It was circulating *Stand Up For America—The Story of George Wallace*—a possible indication of its own political hope for 1968, and a hedge against the failure of its effort to take over the GOP by the time the next Presidential election draws near. It was offering for local screening the film called *Choice,* produced in 1964 by Mothers for a Moral America, and rejected by Senator Goldwater for use in his campaign as "racist" in content. (Hicks of Liberty Lobby called the film a "strong drawing card for fund-raising efforts.")

The fund-raising campaign itself put it to Liberty Lobby's more than 100,000 subscribers in the form of a challenge:

> If we were to raise merely $40,000 more this year than last, we could more than double our lobbying; $100,000 more and we could have a lobbying organization almost equal to that of the AFL-CIO! That is something to work for.

It was clear that an average of $1 from each subscriber would more than achieve the larger goal—and as Hicks himself said in the fund-raising appeal during mid-summer, 1966, "there are hundreds of subscribers who would not miss $5,000—the limit which any person is allowed to contribute to a political organization like LIBERTY LOBBY."

In January, 1967, the organization held what it called the first national convention of its Board of Policy. Listed as speakers, besides Liberty Lobby's Chairman, Curtis Dall, and Hicks himself, were two members of Congress—Republican Rep. Albert Watson of South Carolina, and Democratic Rep. John Rarick, who had been elected only a few months earlier from Louisiana. In addition, there were some Radical Rightist stalwarts on the list of scheduled speakers: J. Evetts Haley, author of the 1964 paperback attack on President Johnson, *A Texan Looks at Lyndon,* who delivered the banquet keynote address entitled "A Texan Revisits Lyndon"; Maj. Arch Roberts, former aide to Gen. Edwin A. Walker, who spoke on "The Impending Demise of the UN," and a number of other ultra-rightists.

Another major speaker was State Sen. John Schmitz of California who was elected in 1964 as an avowed member of The John Birch Society and re-elected in 1966. His speech was an attempt to show that a candidate can win even while running as a committed Right-Winger and an admitted member of the Birch group. Schmitz decried charges of anti-Negroism and anti-Semitism which he said were hurled at Rightists and urged his audience not to let such charges frighten them. Then he quipped that he was about to make a remark about Jews and was sure that much would be made of it by some columnists. He said: "Watch this. The Roman Jews were so happy to get off the hook for the death of Christ that they're thinking of tearing up the mortgage of the Vatican."

Rarick was introduced by Richard Cotten, the anti-Semitic and Radical Rightist broadcaster. The recently-elected Congressman was scheduled to speak on the subject "A Freshman Looks at Congress" but spoke instead on the subject "For Christ and Constitution." His remarks included the assertion that the United States was founded on Christian ideals and that it would survive by going back to Christianity and Christ.

The Washington, D.C., *Post* reported during the convention that Liberty Lobby was "expanding its operations substantially" and that it was "seeking to become a major national organization uniting local right-wing groups."

Carto, the mainspring of Liberty Lobby, was not listed as a speaker and the *Post* noted that he had twice declined interviews with reporters covering the Liberty Lobby gathering. The paper pointed out that Carto had been under attack in the weeks before the convention by columnist Drew Pearson who had quoted from anti-Semitic and anti-Negro letters he attributed to Carto and which he said came from a former Liberty Lobby employee who had defected. Liberty Lobby had unsuccessfully sought to block publication of the letters.

Whatever the details, it was clear at the start of 1967 that Liberty Lobby was pushing forward with anything but thoughts of retreat or retrenchment, and was heavily engaged in a campaign against the proposed U.S.–Soviet consular treaty.

• Rev. Carl McIntire's complex of operations also was branching out as 1967 began. Warning that he was in danger of losing 200 of his more than 600 radio stations carrying the 20th Century Reformation Hour—the heart of his operation—McIntire turned to his faithful supporters for contributions to save the theatened stations and to expand the total to 1,000 across the country. His American Council of Christian Churches was embarked on an expansion program that contemplated the establishment of regional offices across the country; during 1966, offices were opened in Atlanta and Harrisburg, and others were planned for major cities in the Far West and the Midwest. McIntire's *Christian Beacon* newspaper—its domestic circulation 84,700—was being printed in Spanish for distribution in Latin America, and broadcasting operations in the Caribbean also were being launched.

The ACCC continued to wage war against the National Council of Churches, and McIntire's International Council of Christian Churches laid down a steady drumfire of criticism against the World Council of Churches. Meanwhile, McIntire sought to bolster his 15-year-old network of support in Latin America—The Latin American Alliance of Christian Churches with branches in 11 Central and South American countries.

All the while McIntire called for a "New American Society"—a society he envisioned as free of the United Nations, income taxes, civil rights laws, "modern" Protestantism, and the "socialistic, collectivistic, bureaucratic crowd down in Washington."

With an annual gross of at least $3,000,000, McIntire continued to operate Shelton College and his Christian Admiral resort hotel, both on the Atlantic shore at Cape May, N.J.; and late in 1966, he sold land in Northern New Jersey, former site of the college, for $2,200,000.

He had his problems, too. His purchase, in 1965, of radio station WXUR-AM and FM, Media, Pa., led to objections, filed with the Federal Communications Commission, complaining of the heavy overload of Radical Rightist political propagandizing carried over WXUR.

The Pennsylvania House of Representatives adopted a

resolution criticizing the broadcast operation and calling on the FCC to investigate. McIntire staged a series of protest rallies on the Capitol steps in Harrisburg and a series of "cow pasture" rallies across the Keystone State to mobilize his followers against the threat.

But McIntire doesn't worry. Because, as he told his followers in a fund-raising letter, "I do not believe God wants this to happen."

• Billy James Hargis also is convinced that the Almighty stands at his right hand. He has stated that he was "directed by God" to launch the Christian Crusade, and in a recent financial appeal, he exhorted his followers:

> Surely you know by now that Christian Crusade's message is God's message . . . Christian Crusade is God's cause . . . and that to support this cause financially and to pray for this cause, is to serve God in a way pleasing to him.

When the National Council for Civic Responsibility—an organization set up in 1964 to counter Radical Rightist propaganda—folded for lack of funds, Hargis wrote to his flock:

"I see the hand of God in this . . ."

As 1966 opened, Hargis was running a one-million-dollar-a-year operation—and if 1965 contributions to his building fund are included, his gross topped the million-dollar mark by a comfortable margin.

Hargis, a heavy-set man, is a big operator with big dreams, big plans, and big problems. One of his perennial dreams was realized in 1966 with the completion of the Christian Crusade "cathedral" in Tulsa—a $440,000 edifice that was dedicated on August 7, 1966, during the annual convention of the Crusade.

Hargis claims to need $125,000 a month to carry on his radio broadcasting, publishing and tent-show type rallies. In October, he wrote his flock that the Crusade had, during the 1966 summer months, built up an indebtedness of over $100,000, and that its income during September was $39,000 less than its operating expenses.

Now I am asking you to rally around me. Encourage me right now. God knows I need encouragement. If everyone on my mailing list would just pledge something— even if it's $1 or $2 a week, we would have no financial problems . . .

I need some contributions right now and I need them badly . . . No matter how large or small your contribution is, I am praying for a 100% response from this letter . . . Cast your vote "for Christ and against Communism . . ."

In the fall of 1966, Hargis announced a new 12-month program called "Strategy for Awakening," which he said was designed "to awaken the people and to recruit them for Christian anti-Communist service, using the most effective means of communication."

The program, to be implemented "with God's guidance and anointing," amounted to an all-out effort to beef up the Christian Crusade's finances, circulation, and nationwide membership—and all in the trappings of religion. "God, certainly, met with the staff of Christian Crusade," Hargis wrote in the November issue of his magazine, "and gave us ideas, plans and methods . . ."

The "God-given" plans and methods included: raising the circulation figure of *Christian Crusade* by 40,000, and doubling that of the *Weekly Crusader;* concentrating on "super-power stations in metropolitan areas" for the Crusade radio programs (the first indication that Hargis may have been losing some of his far-flung outlets in smaller towns); releasing four new documentary films—attacks on the National Council of Churches, the UN, and the civil rights movement, together with a catch-all called *What You Can Do to Save Your Country.*

Other plans: to add four traveling promoters to the Hargis staff (they would "urge our friends to include Christian Crusade in their wills"); to build up the Torchbearers, the Crusade's youth division; to publish and distribute a number of new books (among them "a sensational book, exploding the Roosevelt myth" by Curtis B. Dall, the former son-in-law of Franklin D. Roosevelt, who now heads Liberty Lobby); and to extend the activities of the Christian Crusade chapters across the country.

Hargis had previously set forth plans for a "chapter" system with striking similarities to that of The John Birch Society. The Hargis manual called for monthly meetings, with discussions of a monthly bulletin, reports of work accomplished, and "members' monthly messages" to be sent to headquarters enclosing sealed contributions—all carbon-copied from Birch Society procedures.

The Christian Crusade chapter structure was, in fact, so closely modeled along Birch Society lines that Robert Welch himself could not have done better if he had set out to mobilize Hargis' fundamentalist followers under his own banner. In any case, the Christian Crusade early in 1967 appeared to be emerging as a kind of fundamentalist adjunct of The John Birch Society—a kind of parallel organization bringing the Birchite line to Hargis' followers with a flavoring more palatable to the true believers in the Bible belt.

Hargis, however, set the dues at half those of the Society —for after all, he has said, "I die a little each time I ask for money."

• "The Lord loveth a cheerful giver," wrote Dr. Fred Schwarz of the Christian Anti-Communism Crusade from his Long Beach, California, headquarters in the fall of 1966. He told his mailing list, "We urgently need an extra $50,000"—for the Schwarz effort to help save Thailand from Communism and for "special schools of anti-Communism for students in Washington, D.C., and on the West Coast during the summer of 1967." Schwarz also told the Crusaders that he wanted to set up televised schools of anti-Communism during 1967, and to maintain his ongoing work in the United States and "21 other countries."

Schwarz's Crusade grossed more than a million dollars in 1961—the first big year of the Radical Right push. Then began a decline that cut the doctor down to less maneuverable size. Even during the excitement of 1964, Schwarz's CACC was obliged to live within an income of $612,000 —a very respectable amount, however reduced.

Nevertheless, a series of emergency financial appeals in 1965 continuously spoke of debts and deficits. In one, Schwarz pleaded:

> Who would benefit most if the Crusade stopped functioning? Who can destroy the Crusade?

He confessed that there were times when he was so sorely tried financially that he was "tempted to go home to my wife and family in Australia and to resume medical practice . . ."

The words of doom apparently succeeded, for by February, 1966, the doctor was able to report that the cause had survived, that the deficit of approximately $50,000 for 1965 had been made up, and that the Crusade had ended the year on a "high financial note." His later report to the Internal Revenue Service showed a total gross for 1965 of more than half-a-million dollars.

During 1966, Schwarz continued to place his financial requirements at $50,000 a month—roughly $600,000 a year. But he bemoaned the fact that his regular pledged support was less than $4,000 a month. In October, 1966, he reported signs of an upturn—but it appeared that he would end the year with lower total proceeds than in 1965.

Like most of the Radical Right's entrepreneurs, Schwarz is an ingenious and durable activist. During 1966, he developed several new techniques to bring the Crusading word to new and untapped audiences around the country, while at the same time carrying forward his travels to various cities for one-night rallies or anti-Communism "schools."

In 1965, Schwarz sought, without marked success, to build a television fund, but during 1966—always flexible —he switched to more easily achievable activity. One project was a series of tape-recorded lectures titled *What Is Communism?*, offered to college radio stations and Crusaders who might wish to start Study Groups using the recordings and Schwarz's book, *You Can Trust The Communists (to be Communists)*, as resource material. Sixty-three college stations put the tapes on the air.

For commercial radio stations, Schwarz devised a series of "public service" spot announcements, plugging a Schwarz booklet (*The Heart, Mind and Soul of Communism*) and other CACC materials. One of the spots featured Janet Greene, an "anti-Communist folk-singer."

The spot announcement project was launched in January, 1966, via a letter to radio stations pointing out the continuing threat of world Communism which, Schwarz warned, "has now conquered more than a thousand million people, over a third of the world's population." In a May, 1966, follow-up letter to stations that had not yet agreed to air the spots, Schwarz pointed out that the purpose was to inform listeners how they could get "authoritative, up-to-the-minute information from the non-political, non-sectarian and non-profit Christian Anti-Communism Crusade."

Schwarz said he would have been happy to have had a response to his initial mailing from 100 stations. The actual response, he said, was far better; he said that 246 stations across the country were airing the CACC announcements. And, he added, "many are also broadcasting our 15-minute programs."

By the latter part of 1966, Schwarz was trying to revamp his organizational format to the needs of 1967. But he was something less of a force on the Radical Right than he was in 1961 when he was hitting city after city with his "schools" and rallies, skimming the financial cream off the top while creating a climate that made it easy for the hard-nosed Birch organizers to move in for recruitment.

• Just as active, though perhaps less flamboyant than the McIntire, Hargis, and Schwarz operations, is the Church League of America. Based in Wheaton, Ill., the CLA is headed by Edgar Bundy, a minister-without-pulpit who is the ideological ally of McIntire in the war against the National and World Councils of Churches. The CLA boasts that it has more than 3,000,000 cross-referenced index cards "on all organizations and individuals who have aided the cause of subversion over a period of years." The Church League also maintains five tons of files of propaganda material issued by what it describes as "left-wing organizations."

In 1966, Bundy acquired the voluminous files maintained for many years by the late J. B. Matthews, a long-time, self-styled expert on Communism and once the research director for the McCarthy investigating committee of the 1950s. It was Matthews' 1953 public charge of Communist infiltration into the nation's churches that heralded the widespread barrage of similar accusations now emanating from the Radical Right of the 1960s. During the last years of his life, Matthews headed research for the Church League of America. He died in July, 1966.

The Matthews files, said by Bundy to be valued at $150,000, were to be ensconced at the CLA headquarters at Wheaton, and Bundy announced plans for expansion of the League's colonial-style headquarters building, in part (he wrote in his plea for a $100,000 building fund) to house and provide maximum security for the Matthews collection.

CLA carries out a wide variety of activities that are standard for many of the organizations of the Radical Right. It offers a thick catalogue of publications and training aids for Americans who share its view of America and the world. It issues a regular publication called *News and Views,* as well as special reports, pamphlets and booklets, a long list of tape recordings, and a variety of films and film strips.

Besides the 200 tapes offered radio stations and interested citizens, the CLA plugs several books written by Bundy himself on his favorite theme, the more recent being *How the Communists Use Religion* and *Apostles of Deceit.*

But there are activities in which CLA is somewhat unique. It offers "one-day counter-subversive seminars," claiming to be "the pioneer organization in the United States for presenting counter-subversive seminars in city after city since 1937."

The League boasted that "later organizations have sought to duplicate the Church League's method, but the majority of these have dealt in generalizations and theories, rather than in specifics." It added:

> The Church League of America deals with specific documentation involving hundreds of names in individuals, organizations, publications and institutions. We locate the enemy and tell how he works . . .

To hold a seminar, a local group must mobilize at least 75 persons, each of whom pays $10; this entitles them not only to the seminar, but to a kit of documentation and a year's subscription to *News and Views* and the League's *Special Report Service.* High school and college seminar enrollees "can be sponsored for $5 each."

Another way in which CLA is unique: any contributor of $10 a year has the privilege of securing documented information, via a CLA name-check, on any suspected left-wing individual, organization, publication, or institution.

Edgar Bundy maintains a rigorous speaking schedule that crisscrosses the country each year, averaging almost two appearances a week. He broadcasts his message on a small network of 12 or 14 stations mostly in the West—while sailing along on an income that is in the neighborhood of a quarter of a million dollars a year.

In the fall of 1966, Bundy was invited to South Africa, citadel of racial apartheid, for a series of speeches sponsored by South Africa's National Council to Combat Communism, also known as Antikom. A dispatch from Johannesburg to *The New York Times* reported that a few weeks after Bundy's return to the United States, echoes of his visit were still "reverberating around the country" and that pamphlets of his speeches were being prepared for widespread distribution. Antikom was reported to be arranging another visit for Bundy in 1967.

Bundy's basic theme, the *Times* said, was "communism in the churches," and was well-received by some church elements in South Africa. It was noted that on an earlier visit, Bundy had boasted that his book, *Collectivism in the Churches,* had been instrumental in causing the Afrikaans church to withdraw from the World Council of Churches. Bundy described the WCC as "permeated with Communist clergymen from the Soviet Union and its satellite states," and as including "many leading leftists and Christ-denying clergymen from the Western world."

The *Times* quoted an unnamed "leading American journalist in South Africa" as saying that "Bundy may be a minor crank in the States, but he sure gets the red-carpet treatment here."

• Stirring up the white backlash and plugging for a third party movement—with George Wallace of Alabama for President in 1968—are Kent and Phoebe Courtney, until 1966 the Radical Right's most important (perhaps only) husband-and-wife team. The Courtneys, who separated in August of that year, maintained headquarters in New Orleans. Phoebe edits *The Independent American,* a newspaper mish-mash of reprints from other Rightist pens, and a series of shrill tracts called *Tax Fax.* Kent is National Chairman of the Conservative Society of America. And they have also been proprietors of the Pelican Printing Co., Inc.

The Independent American is a clearinghouse of news, opinions, and activities on the Radical Right, and is heavily political. In the fall of 1966, *The Independent American* heralded the formation of a "Wallace for President Club" and urged all who wished to form local units to write Kent Courtney at P.O. Box 4254, New Orleans—the same P.O. Box used by Pelican Printing.

Another segment of the Courtney apparatus has been Free Men Speak, Inc., which in the fall of 1966 was taking orders for Dr. Douglass' novel, *The Eagle's Feather*. Douglass is associated with Kent Courtney's Conservative Society of America, and Courtney, like Douglass, devoutly follows the Birchite line on many issues. Free Men Speak blurbed the Douglass novel for shock effect:

> "Have a Coke!" Today Wren, big-boned, bronze and beautiful, hurled a flaming Molotov cocktail at the U. N. tank. The United Nations, like a trained watchdog gone mad, had turned on its benefactor, the United States. In the 1970's the United Nations had become a world dictatorship—and the United States had to fight for its life to survive against the monster it had fed so well.

The titles of some of the *Tax Fax* leaflets that poured from New Orleans during 1966 suggest the Courtney line: *What's Behind Race Riots?; Subversion in the Schools; Foreign Aid Aids Reds; Is Your Home Really Yours?*

No one is safe from the Radical Right—not even former Vice-President Richard M. Nixon, the man who exposed Alger Hiss and whose credentials as an anti-Communist have never been questioned in responsible quarters. Kent Courtney's Conservative Society of America recently published a leaflet entitled *Nixon in '68?* with the revealing subtitle, "An Exposé of the Leftwing Record of Richard Nixon, Possible Presidential Candidate of the Liberal-Controlled Republican Party."

The Omaha *World-Herald* reported on October 30, 1966, that the anti-Nixon leaflet had been mailed to more than 1,500 residents of Omaha, and quoted Kent Courtney as declaring:

> I don't see how otherwise well-adjusted people can possibly ignore the fact that Nixon is a dedicated internationalist who belongs to the same organization as Senator Jacob Javits and Vice-President Hubert Humphrey.
>
> The organization I mean is the Communist-accommodating Council on Foreign Relations whose aims and purposes as revealed by their own literature are parallel to the long-range plans of the International Communist Conspiracy.

The Courtney attack on Nixon was summed up by the sub-headings carried in its text:

"Nixon and Big Government"; "Nixon's Extremism on Civil Rights"; "Nixon a Member of the N.A.A.C.P."; "Nixon and Martin Luther King"; "Nixon and Red Cuba"; "Nixon's Phony Anti-Communism."

The leaflet was available from CSA at standard bulk rates—20 for a dollar, 1,000 for $35 (postage prepaid).

Also available from CSA were "Win With Wallace in 1968" lapel buttons, at 25¢ apiece, 10 for a dollar, and "Wallace for President" license plates at $1.25 each (postpaid).

For Kent and Phoebe Courtney, politics has always been a full-time business.

• It's not much different with Dan Smoot of Dallas, whose publication *The Dan Smoot Report* and whose broadcasts over radio and television have made him a factor on the Radical Right—a status he has earned in the years since he struck out on his own after leaving the employ of H. L. Hunt. Smoot had been the radio voice for Hunt's Facts Forum broadcasts, predecessor organization of the 1950s to Hunt's current Life Line Foundation.

Like Courtney, Smoot views the Council on Foreign

81

Relations as part of "the invisible government which sets the major policies of the federal government . . ." In his 1962 book, *The Invisible Government,* Smoot wrote of the CFR:

> I am convinced that the objective of this invisible government is to convert America into a socialist state and then make it a unit in a one-world socialist system.

Smoot takes a back seat to no one on the Radical Right in warning against the current trends in Washington. In September, 1966, for instance, he summed up the record of the 89th Congress by declaring:

> In one year (1965), the 89th Congress, under President Johnson's drive for "consensus," enacted unconstitutional, socialistic legislation more damaging to the cause of freedom than *all* legislation enacted during the administrations of Franklin D. Roosevelt, Harry S. Truman, Dwight D. Eisenhower, and John F. Kennedy.

Smoot's uncompromising stands earned him the support of the late Dallas Bedford Lewis, California pet food manufacturer, who sponsored Smoot on radio and television and assured the Dallas propagandist of a niche in the forefront of the nation's Radical Right complex. And in 1966, when Lewis died, he bequeathed one million dollars to Smoot, and another million to Pepperdine College in Los Angeles, "providing they have honored Dan Smoot with a doctorate degree during my life time or within six months after my death."

Pepperdine turned down the bequest. Lewis also left a million to The John Birch Society provided that the money was available after the estate was liquidated and all other bequests made. He further stipulated that Birch Society Public Relations Director John Rousselot would have to be with the Society and agree to direct the use of the funds "in the work of finding and exposing Communism in the United States."

To his brother, Horace E. Lewis, the pet food manufacturer left "Ten dollars and my best wishes."

Toward the end of 1966, Lewis' widow filed suit against Smoot and the Birch Society claiming that they unduly influenced her late husband in the preparation of his will. She charged that it "is not and never was" the will of her deceased spouse.

Further complicating the situation was the announcement by Rousselot, early in 1967, that he was resigning his post as Birch Society Public Relations Director, to take effect in the spring of the year. Rousselot said he was going into private business, but that he would continue to work for the Society as a volunteer.

The Rousselot announcement came only a few weeks after Thomas J. Davis, the East Coast Public Relations Manager of the Society, had quit—also to go into private business.

Propaganda and Recruitment

The incessant propaganda deluge which pours forth from the Liberty Lobbyists, the Schwarz and Hargis Crusades, the McIntires, the Bundys, the Courtneys and the Smoots is aided and abetted by less well-known activists, some of whom have emerged in the last few years.

These include West Coast fundamentalists such as Rev. Bob Wells and Rev. W. S. McBirnie, and a legion of other individuals, organizations and publications scattered across the country.

Together with the more imposing establishments of the Radical Right, they comprise a movement that creates the ideological climate in which recruitment can take place and that makes easier the organizing activities of groups such as The John Birch Society, the major membership apparatus of the Radical Right.

How many members came to the Society's ranks after repeated exposure to the writings and the rantings of

Radical Right propagandists will probably never be known. But it is a fact of life that such urgent and insistent voices pre-condition many thousands of Americans for more active participation in the war against "the conspiracy." The paid coordinators of the Birch Society, backed by thousands of zealous Society members and with membership blanks in hand, follow the tent shows and the pamphleteers of the Radical Right with results that will now be set forth in detail.

Part Two

THE
JOHN BIRCH
SOCIETY

An updated and expanded
revision of *Report on the
John Birch Society 1966*

CHAPTER SEVEN

Fantastic Measures

The strange dream has come a long way since those two long December days in an Indianapolis hotel in 1958. During those days, eleven Americans sat and listened while a twelfth, a retired Massachusetts candymaker, delivered a breathless monologue picturing the United States of America in the grip of the "Communist Conspiracy" and proposing a far-reaching and spectacular means of releasing that grip.

In that room, The John Birch Society was founded. The long monologue, recorded and published, became its *Blue Book*. The monologist became its leader—its "dynamic personal leader" who said that those thousands who would join him would do so "primarily because they believe in me and what I am doing and are willing to accept my leadership . . ."

Robert Welch and his followers have since become the central fact of the Radical Right in America. They are permanently organized across the whole country at the grass-roots level, and they have begun to insinuate themselves into our national life.

Among the major organizations of the Radical Right, only The John Birch Society has a nationwide paid staff of organizers and public relations men, a membership active and activated, a permanent recruiting program, a tightly controlled and generally efficient centralized direction, and a financial income which enables it to maintain its nation-wide organizational structure.

Starting from scratch at the beginning of 1959, the Society has grown to a membership of about 80,000 in some 4,000 chapters across the country. Since 1963 its membership has almost doubled; its cash income more than quadrupled.

The 80,000 membership, directed by Founder Robert Welch from the Belmont, Mass., headquarters of the Society, just about equals the membership of the Communist Party when the Communists were at the peak of their strength in the United States in 1944. The Society is, in fact, a movement and a propaganda and recruitment "apparatus" on the Far Right that is comparable to the Communist "apparatus" on the Far Left in the 1930s and 1940s. The earlier movement of the Radical Left preached Communism while today's Birch Society, on the Radical Right, claims to preach anti-Communism. But in terms of organizational concept, structure, and tactics, the similarities between the two operations often appear more persuasive than the differences.

Infiltration Tactics

The Birchers, like the Communists of 20 and 30 years ago, have burrowed their way into the fabric and the grass roots of American life and it is already clear that it will take a major effort by responsible forces to root them out.

The overwhelming majority of Birch members still conceal their membership in the Society.

The Birch Society today has spawned scores of front groups, formed to lure unsuspecting Americans into the Birch orbit and to ripen them for eventual membership in the Society by enlisting their support for limited and high-sounding causes with whose slogans, at least, few would disagree.

The Birchers have already infiltrated the American political party structure and in some areas have secured footholds at the precinct level and a measurable degree of influence in various arms of the political party apparatus.

Like the Communists, the Birchers have established local book stores all across the country which serve as distribution centers for Birchite and other Radical Right propaganda, as gathering places for Radical Rightists, and as focal points for Birchite activity, much as Communist bookstores in the 1930s and 1940s served a similar function.

The Birchers have available a large stable of speakers, ready, willing and able to travel anywhere in the country to address local meetings, sponsored not only by Birch groups, but by local civic, political and service organizations as well.

Like the Communists, the Birchers have set up their own publishing house and are not only pumping their own books and pamphlets into the nation's ideological bloodstream, but are reprinting the propaganda of like-minded Radical Rightists for wholesale distribution to their own network of bookstores and to bookstores operated by other Far Rightists as well.

Cell Structure

The Birchers are organized into small units designed to operate as isolated islands, impervious to penetration by outsiders. The Communists called these units "cells"; the Birchers call them chapters.

The Birch membership is supervised and directed by paid professional organizers, set up on an area, state and local basis. These professionals were called "organizers" by the Communists; the Birchers call them "coordinators."

Like the Communists, the Birchers get their official "line" from a central headquarters. The Communists got their "line" from Moscow, via National Party headquarters; the Birchers get their line from Founder Welch via Birch headquarters in Belmont.

Like the Communists, the Birchers brook no deviation from the "line." The Communists expelled deviationists; the Birchers do the same, careful as always to refund pre-paid dues on a pro-rata basis.

(Bircher applicants abjectly fill out a membership form that is a resignation signed in advance, agreeing when they join that the Society can drop them at any time and without any necessary explanation for doing so.)

Like the Communists, Birchers are urged to take an active role in political and community organizations. For instance, Robert Welch, in 1960, urged his followers to join their local PTAs at the start of the school year, to get their "conservative friends to do likewise," and to "go to work" to take the PTAs over.

An Ideological Cadre

The Birchers seek to accomplish their purposes by enlisting the support of a dedicated, zealous, disciplined and thoroughly-indoctrinated ideological cadre of workers—distinctly a minority in their areas of operation, whether local, regional or national.

The Birch Society is not designed to mobilize anything close to a majority of the American national population. Like Lenin, Robert Welch of The John Birch Society believes that a dedicated minority, which knows what it wants, can move mountains.

The Birchers' target is the American mind. Like the Communists, their aim is to change—and eventually to control—American political thinking. Their ultimate goal is political influence and political power.

The Communists of two and three decades ago pointed to the growing and—to them—extremist activities of Big Capital. According to the Communists, capitalism, then in its "last stages," was evolving into fascism and imperialism. In the same spirit, Robert Welch analyzed, in mid-1965, the development of the forces against which he has allegedly aligned his Society:

> (1) The Communist conspiratorial apparatus is now closing in, with every conceivable pressure and deception, on all remaining resistance to the establishment of its police state over our own country; (2) the only existing force that has any possible chance of preventing the completion of these Communist plans is The John Birch Society; (3) we have no chance of stopping and reversing the long patient progress of this conspiracy except—exactly as stated in the Blue Book six years ago—by measures which are *fantastic* enough to be *realistic* in proportion to the danger . . .

"Fantastic" measures—some of them admitted by Welch to be "mean and dirty"—have become the trademark of Birch Society activity. And the wheels now are spinning. The active search for new members, after an initial policy of quiet recruitment, has been pushed with increasingly high pressure since 1963. All during which time the Birchers have worked to clean up their public image while Welch engaged in some hard-headed planning for future political influence.

Membership

The membership "explosion" that has vastly increased Birch membership rolls since the 1964 national political conventions was the result of many factors. Most of them were related to the Presidential election campaign in which Birchers and other such extremists were active, welcomed, defended and, to a certain extent, triumphant. At the Republican convention, the Birch Society covered itself with a kind of respectability. Birchers misused the campaign as a vehicle to spread their own political propaganda and to recruit new members.

Many Americans were swept into the Birch ranks on the

emotional tide of the campaign period. Many others joined after Election Day, when the frustration of defeat made them ripe for recruitment and when the Birch Society's post-election appeal to this group was summed up in the simple slogan: *"Now* Will You Join The John Birch Society?"

From August through December, 1964, the Society set new membership records and early in 1965, the growth was described by a jubilant Welch as having been of "geometric" proportions.

In 1965 and into 1966, membership growth continued, but the rate of growth leveled off during 1966. Several factors were at work. For example:

• Many who joined during the exciting days of the 1964 campaign found the Society demanded too much of their time, energy and dedication. They either drifted away or were dropped from membership by the Society itself, for like the Communists, the Birch Society does not tolerate "dead wood" for long.

• Some of the 1964 recruits—especially Goldwater enthusiasts frustrated by the defeat of their champion—found the Society too radical for their basically conservative viewpoints. They walked away along with still others who found it too "moderate" or too "educational."

Birch Society recruitment canceled out these losses and if net membership gains in 1966 were less than sensational, there was no indication of any net loss.

Those who remained faithful to Welch's leadership in early 1967 were, for the most part, the zealous, the dedicated, and the indoctrinated—eager to carry out the monthly instructions sent to them by Welch from the Society's headquarters in Massachusetts.

The California Reports

The Birch Society continues to distribute (in packets designed for the indoctrination of prospective members) the report of a 1963 investigation by the California Senate Fact-Finding Subcommittee on Un-American Activities. It found the organization to be neither secret, subversive nor anti-Semitic. Apparently because of the wide circulation of this 1963 report by the Birch Society, a second report was issued by the same committee in 1965. For understandable reasons, it has been ignored by the Birch Society.

The more recent report found that Robert Welch's organization "has attracted a lunatic fringe that is now assuming serious proportions" and has been "beset by an influx of emotionally unstable people, some of whom have been prosecuted in the courts for their hoodlum tactics in disrupting meetings, and heckling speakers with whom they disagree."

The committee's 1965 report concluded:

> We are more critical of the Society now than we were then for the reason that it has, in our opinion, merited such criticism by reason of its activities exemplified by the irresponsible articles by a member of its National Council, the re-publication of "The Politician," the inexcusable actions of its minority of irresponsible members, and a dangerous increase of anti-Semitism among a minority of the membership.

The members of the Birch Society are believers in the conspiracy theory of history, and in *absolute political truth* which they alone claim to possess. It is through the conspiracy theory of recent American history that fear is aroused—fear, the essential ingredient of extremist strength. The operating premise of The John Birch Society, like that of the Communists, is that over all of our lives and over all the events of our time, there rules a powerful and protected establishment, perpetuated by a secret conspiracy of vast dimensions. To the Birchers it is Communism—by which they mean the "establishment" of the last years, including the American Government, whether controlled by Republicans or Democrats, whether directed by· liberals or conservatives.

93

The John Birch Society has grown in direct proportion to the growth which its Founder sees in the power and influence of "the enemy." Welch has said his organization's chances of success in saving the country have increased from 1 in 10 in 1958 to 1 in 4. Yet, paradoxically, he and his Society claim that in the same period, "Communist influence and control" in the United States increased from 20-40% in 1958 to 60-80% today.

It is to fighting this enemy "control"—in the Federal government, in our two major political parties, in schools and churches and town councils—that Welch's Society and its loyal cadre claim to be firmly dedicated.

CHAPTER EIGHT

The War Against Civil Rights

As The John Birch Society has grown, the movement that seeks justice and equality for America's Negro citizens has become more and more the focal point for the Birchers' assault on democracy.

In 1966, as white indifference, Negro impatience, and wide economic inequities—along with the rise of black extremism—brought racial riots and white backlash to the forefront of America's mind, the Birchers could watch the awful inflammation of sore spots they themselves had rubbed raw with propaganda. For several years the Society had made the civil rights movement the chief target of its peculiar counter-conspiracy, nursing and nurturing an incipient backlash through the manipulation of long-standing prejudices and newly-created fears of alleged Red advances.

The assault began with the publication, in 1965, of a pamphlet by Welch himself which laid down the ideological line. Five hundred thousand copies of *Two Revolutitions At Once,* the 16-page document previously mentioned, were distributed to the Birch army across the country—100 copies to every Birch Society cell.

In mobilizing his troops, Welch made it crystal-clear that the campaign upon which they were embarking was the single most important undertaking of The John Birch Society in its entire seven-year history.

"Fully expose the 'civil rights' fraud," said Welch in May, 1965, "and you will break the back of the Communist conspiracy."

In *Two Revolution At Once,* Welch set forth his view that the Negro civil rights movement in America was part of a world-wide, Communist-dominated, anti-colonialism revolution that used the slogans of freedom, independence and self-determination. At the same time, he said, it was part of the Communist-led revolutionary movement against capitalism in the United States itself.

In his analysis, Welch likened the Negro rights movement in the United States to various "national liberation fronts" in Asia and Africa which in his view have been sparked by Communist terror tactics. The relationship had been revealed, Welch said, in a booklet published by the American Communists in 1928. Called *American Negro Problems,* it referred to the Southern Negroes as "virtually a colony within the body of the United States of America," and called for the establishment of a "Negro Soviet Republic" in the South.

In fact, this 38-year-old Red propaganda line was repudiated by the Communist Party's 1959 convention—because it had already died in the Red failure to win the American Negro to the Communist cause.

The Birch Society, nevertheless, continues to distribute thousands of copies of the 1928 Communist booklet to support its theme—that the efforts for civil rights equality and for racial desegregation are Communist-inspired and subversive.

Another Red booklet—published in 1935 and entitled *Negroes in a Soviet America*—has also been distributed by the Birch Society. It was originally reprinted by the National Economic Council under its late founder, Merwin K. Hart, a well-known American anti-Semite. Before his death a few years ago, Hart was the leader of Birch Society

Chapter 26 in New York; his publications were recommended by Welch to Birch Society members in its early days.

In the June, 1965, *Bulletin,* Welch said:

> Our task must be simply to make clear that the movement known as 'civil rights' is Communist-plotted, Communist-controlled, and in fact . . . serves only Communist purposes. So let's keep our own activities and efforts concentrated on this central undertaking.

Ideological Weapons

Welch mobilized many weapons for the ideological warfare against the civil rights movement. One was a book published by the Birchers' own Western Islands Co. Written by Alan Stang of the Birch stable of writers, it was called *It's Very Simple,* and was essentially a popularized version of the Welch ideology on the Communist character of the civil rights movement. The book had an initial printing of 100,000 copies and sold out in the first few weeks. An additional 200,000 were printed soon thereafter.

Stang wrote that America's race problem and the effort of the civil rights movement to end it were both planned by the Communists, built up by the Communists and, most important, conducted by the Communists. Describing the Civil Rights Act of 1964 as a major step toward a Washington dictatorship, Stang concluded his polemic by declaring:

> I accuse the Rev. Dr. [Martin Luther] King of being in effect one of the country's most influential workers for Communism and *against* the Negroes . . . I accuse President Kennedy and President Johnson of knowing this but nevertheless, not only closing their eyes to it, but lending a hand. I therefore accuse them both of having betrayed their oath of office.

Birch ads declared that the Negroes' problem was exaggerated, that the civil rights movement was not simply "infiltrated" by Communists, but actually "created" by them. A postcard pictured a man identified by the Birchers as the founder of the civil rights movement. They described him as a Hungarian Communist who used such names as Joseph Pogany, John Schwartz, Joseph Lang and John Pepper. They said he arrived in the United States in 1922 and in 1928 wrote the pamphlet, *American Negro Problems,* which laid down the Red line for establishment of the Negro Revolutionary Movement. Aside from the dubious Welchian history, the drawing of Pogany-Schwartz-Lang-Pepper was reminiscent of some of the viciously anti-Jewish caricatures that appeared in *Der Stuermer* during the Nazi era in Germany and of similar caricatures that have been circulated in anti-Semitic ideological circles in the United States.

These materials were added to the arsenal of anti-civil rights propaganda that the Birch Society had been using for some time. Its Civil Rights Packet already included *Color, Communism and Common Sense* by the late Negro ex-Communist, Manning Johnson, and various reprints, all hewing to the Birch line on the civil rights movement as a Communist manifestation.

Statements by Birch Society leaders that the civil rights movement was "plotted" or "created" by the Communists have been ironically contradicted in an official publicity release from the Society's own American Opinion Speakers Bureau. The release states that Lola Belle Holmes, a former FBI informant in the Communist Party, "carried out orders from Moscow to gain control of the 'civil rights' movement." It would seem that "Moscow" should have been smarter than to waste time trying to "gain control" in a movement allegedly Communist from the start.

The TACT Committees

The campaign for a nationwide attack was created by Welch in July, 1965, with a proposed new and major approach to exposure of the "fraud" known as "civil rights." He called for "the setting up throughout the country of hundreds of local or regional *ad hoc* committees for the specific purpose of telling the truth about the civil turmoil." Anticipating that they would come to be known as TACT—Truth About Civil Turmoil—he gave the shorthand name his blessing.

TACT front groups sprang up and swung immediately into high gear, distributing literature, holding meetings, sponsoring lectures by American Opinion speakers, buying full-page ads in local newspapers, and peppering the letters-to-the-editor columns with Birch propaganda exposing the "truth about civil turmoil."

Welch's choice of the Communist-style front-group technique worked admirably. Many non-Birchite Rightists and conservatives were lured into making common cause with the Birchers against the civil rights movement. In many localities, even the newspapers and other media of public information were at first unaware that the TACT committees were Birch fronts. For example:

• In Fort Wayne, Ind., the *News Sentinel* reported the formation of the local TACT Committee and merely noted that it had "been formed to provide information about past instances of civil turmoil in order to prevent recurrences." There was not a hint in the news report of the TACT group's real sponsorship.

• In the suburban Glenview-Northbrook area of Chicago, where a TACT Committee was formed, the local newspaper reported that the committee chairman had said "that the group, conservative in nature, is not connected with any organization." Yet the group's own newspaper advertisement was signed: "The TACT Committee of Northbrook & Glenbrook Division of the John Birch Society."

But the TACT Committees around the country were not the only fronts spearheading the Birch Society's ideological warfare against civil rights:

• The "Detroit Committee for the Prevention of Civil Disorder" listed the same post office box number as the local Birchite "Support Your Local Police" organization, and the same individual was listed as chairman of both.

• In La Puente, Calif., "Citizens for the Support of Law and Order" seized on the Watts riots in Los Angeles, in the summer of 1965, to distribute a flyer captioned "Now Will You Believe?" It was, in effect, an advertisement for Stang's book and bore the Birch Society's "Support Your Local Police" emblem.

• A woman in Whittier, Calif., received a letter from the "Committee for Better Understanding" which listed a post office box in racially troubled Selma, Ala. The letter ended with: "Yours for less government, more individual responsibility and a better world"—the slogan of The John Birch Society.

While waging war against the civil rights movement, The John Birch Society has, at the same time, diligently sought to create a public image of itself as friendly to Negroes. A mainstay of the Birch Speakers Bureau has been Mrs. Julia Brown, a Negro lady who had once been a Communist and later an informant for the government. Others have been the aforementioned Lola Belle Holmes, Leonard Patterson, and George Schuyler, the Negro newspaperman. Birch spokesmen go out of their way to make it clear that the Society has Negro members. As part of the campaign to rid itself of any anti-Negro stigma, the Society has established a Manning Johnson Scholarship for Negro students.

During 1966, the Society began sponsoring a series of "seminars" featuring a panel of its Negro speakers. In Denver, for example, on March 19, the panel appeared under the innocent-sounding sponsorship of the "Denver Committee to Improve Racial Relations." The title lured many of the unsuspecting to a program of undiluted Birchite propaganda.

In Seattle, suspicion of the civil rights movement was peddled by "The Greater Seattle Council for Racial Harmony."

"Anarchy USA"

In mid-1966, the Society produced a two-reel, 75-minute anti-civil rights film entitled *Anarchy USA*—an audio-visual version of Welch's pamphlet, *Two Revolutions at Once.* Describing the film in the August, 1966, *Bulletin,* Welch said:

> It shows how the agitation and rioting now being promoted in this country under the banner of 'civil rights' follows exactly the same pattern and purposes as similar programs under equally deceptive banners which were carried out by the Communists in Cuba and in Algeria —as well as in many other countries.

Welch suggested that the film was "particularly suitable for activities of a TACT Committee" and urged them to obtain it and "start showing it at all feasible opportunities."

By the start of 1967, there were some 260 prints available and more being made. The price was $125 but some groups not affiliated with the Birch Society could get the film free of charge.

Anarchy USA was widely shown around the country— most often by the Birch-front TACT units, but occasionally by other local organizations or by private individuals. The film does not carry any imprimatur, Birch Society or otherwise, so that local viewers not familiar with the Society or its operations have not always been aware that they are watching Birch Society propaganda.

Non-Birchite observers who have seen the film agree that it is dangerously effective. Milwaukee *Journal* reporter Mildred Freese who attended a local screening, concluded:

> *Anarchy USA* is skillfully done . . . It weaves together

a variety of pictures and sounds to carry forth its purpose of labeling the civil rights movement as Communist, with the Rev. Martin Luther King as its Lucifer.

Reporter Freese added that as the viewer is shown uprisings in Algeria, Cuba and China, and then is returned to the United States, the narrator keeps repeating that "as it was in Cuba and China, so it is in the United States," and repeats again and again that the Communists have a five-point program for takeover: find an issue to divide the people, create the appearance of popular support among the people, neutralize the opposition, get the masses stirred up and thus precipitate mob violence, and make others think it is a revolution.

Late in 1966, Welch announced production by the Society of a film strip called *Show Biz in the Streets.* Available for $30, the 34-minute film strip would demonstrate, Welch said, "how the same characters show up all over the United States, to foment and lead these 'spontaneous demonstrations' which so often turn into riots."

Exploiting Racial Tensions

The Birchers seek to exploit racial tensions, unrest and disorders for their own purposes. As noted, 48 hours after the Watts riots in Los Angeles in the summer of 1965, Birch chapters were mobilized—via a directive to all area chapter leaders—for an intensive anti-civil-rights-movement drive to exploit the white reaction to the outburst of violence and disorder. During 1965, Birch propaganda had much to say about the Selma Civil Rights March—some of it indistinguishable from the outpourings of openly racist organizations in the Deep South.

In the June, 1965, issue of *American Opinion,* writer Jim Lucier described the Selma march as having been "organized by the International Conspiracy of Evil." An unsigned article in the July issue purported to describe what happened "when a horde of termites from all over the country, led by half-crazed ministers and professors, swarmed over the small town of Selma, Ala., in a typical demonstration of Communist activism."

It would be hard to finger such explosive "educational" prose as a direct cause of violence in the South, but it is equally difficult to see in it any indication of an attempt to restore the racial harmony that Robert Welch, born and raised on a North Carolina farm, claims existed in the past.

Welch has described such visions. In the June, 1965, *Bulletin*, he wrote of "that huge reservoir of good will between the races that was such a happy circumstance of American life only two decades ago." And in a recent television interview he saw that period (a time of Negro second-class citizenship and enforced Jim Crow vassalage) as having included "a very, very tiny amount of injustice."

Such may be the cornerstone of the racial attitudes The John Birch Society is building; the "happy circumstance" was one of segregation and inequality.

The quarrel of the Birch Society with the concept of Negro equality goes far deeper than mere questions of politics and methods, or even of the alleged Communist character of the civil rights movement itself.

• In *The Blue Book* of the Society, Welch decried democracy as "merely a deceptive phrase, a weapon of demagoguery, and a perennial fraud." In a footnote he added that democracy was "the worst of all forms of government."

• Jim Lucier, a frequent contributor to *American Opinion*, argued in the June, 1965, issue that (1) voting is not one of the basic rights of a human being; (2) there is no direct relationship between voting and freedom; and (3) the doctrine of majority rule is alien to American political tradition and ideals.

• In the November, 1964, issue, Professor Revilo P. Oliver, then a member of the Society's National Council and once described by Welch as "quite possibly the world's

103

greatest living scholar," wrote that it was a lie that the races are equal.

• In the February, 1965, issue, National Council member Tom Anderson wrote that "the right to discriminate is the right to choose and the right to choose is the essence of liberty."

Tainted Sources

Welch and those who wage war at his side are not always careful about the sources they cite to back up their contentions:

In the June, 1965, Birch *Bulletin*, for instance, Welch quoted "the long and prophetically accurate December, 1956 Special Report of the American Flag Committee." The American Flag Committee had predicted nine years earlier, he said, that 1965 was marked by the Communists as the target year for agitation for Negro voting rights. Welch devoted five full pages of the *Bulletin* to this report, and cited the American Flag Committee in five separate references.

The American Flag Committee was, in fact, a small-time propaganda outfit run by W. Henry MacFarland, Jr., of Philadelphia, an outspoken anti-Semite who toured the country some years ago with Gerald Smith, the anti-Jewish rabble-rouser. MacFarland cooperated with the late Conde McGinley, Jew-baiting publisher of *Common Sense*, and with the gutter-level, racist and anti-Semitic National Rennaissance Party, headed by James Madole of New York, a minor pamphleteer and street corner agitator.

Welch's members had no way of knowing that two of the organizations founded by MacFarland before he created the American Flag Committee were included in the U. S. Attorney General's list of subversive organizations. One was MacFarland's Nationalist Action League; the other, the Committee for Nationalist Action.

The July-August, 1965, issue of *American Opinion* gave

source credit, in an evaluation of racial questions, to *The Councilor,* the hate sheet edited in Shreveport, Louisiana, by Ned Touchstone as the house organ of the White Citizens' Councils of Louisiana.

And the Councils themselves, source of much of the openly racist propaganda against civil rights that regularly floods the Southern states, deserve more than a passing reference in the Birch story.

Dr. Medford Evans, an official in the Citizens' Councils of America, headquartered in Jackson, Miss., has been listed as a member of the Society's Committee of Endorsers, and is a contributing editor of Robert Welch's *American Opinion* magazine. The January, 1967, issue of *The Citizen,* official Council magazine, announced that Evans would serve as its managing editor.

Louis Hollis is the national executive director of the Citizens' Councils, and William Simmons the editor of *The Citizen.* According to the Los Angeles *Times,* "Hollis said both he and Simmons are John Birch Society members and that he felt an affinity exists between the two organizations . . ."

This affinity may have been demonstrated when the White Citizens' Councils' 1966 National Convention at Chattanooga was addressed by Oliver, then a member of the Birch Society's National Council.

Purposes

The stated purpose of the Society's anti-civil rights campaign was set forth by Welch in a July, 1965, pamphlet entitled *A Stick of Dynamite.* The Society, he wrote, was not strong enough to fight a war, but it was strong enough to fight a battle and have a chance of success if it concentrated its forces on one front.

What are the true purposes of the Society's all-out attack on the civil rights movement?

First, it offers a tremendous field for nationwide membership activity and for recruitment through front groups. Second, it is a logical preliminary to the exploitation of emotional white backlash for openly political purposes, which, as will be seen, are at the heart of the whole concept of The John Birch Society.

What is most significant is that toward these political purposes, the Society capitalizes on the tensions and grief attending today's racial problems—on neighborhood ferment, on fears and prejudices, on the violence that may flare up when frustration and resentment are nudged by extremist ideas of any sort. In 1966, white backlash became a reality in the wake of race riots and similar disturbances —some, though not all of them, spurred on by Negro extremists who themselves were exploiting whatever natural bitterness could be found to exploit. It was a backlash carefully nurtured in recent years by Birchite and other Radical Right propaganda.

In short, the Birch Society's purposes of propaganda and recruitment, and its somewhat deeper goals of political influence, have been served—as the Communists have always tried to serve theirs—by the callous exploitation of human tears and turmoil. Birch Society Public Relations Director John Rousselot stated with obvious pride in September, 1966, for example, that the Hough riots in Cleveland in July had noticeably swelled the local Birch Society membership. Birch efforts to exploit the tragic riots in American cities apparently paid off in Cleveland.

CHAPTER NINE

The
John Birch
Society Line

The Birch propaganda line on the civil rights struggle—that it is directed by the international Communist conspiracy, or, more mysteriously, by an "International Conspiracy of Evil"—is part and parcel of the conspiracy theory of history adapted by Welch from the bizarre, discredited myths told by extremist pseudo historians through all of modern times. The Birch Society leadership has refined it, modernized it, and disseminated it to an incredibly wide audience throughout the United States.

In its present state, this conspiracy theory, as the official propaganda line of The John Birch Society, looks like this—and added comment would be superfluous:

Washington has been taken over! By which we mean that Communist influences are now in full working control of the Federal Government. (From *The Time Has Come,* written by Robert Welch, admittedly "For The John Birch Society")

. . . And everywhere in the world the State Department is doing everything it can to advance the global Communist conquest. (*Ibid.*)

Americans can expect only defeat so long as they are commanded by their enemies. (*American Opinion,* July-August, 1965)

Communist domination of many departments of the federal government is too obvious to require much comment. (*Ibid.*)

The efforts of the Warren Gang to produce a tidal wave of violence and crime are accomplishing their purpose. (*Ibid.*)

In November, 1964 forty-two million supporters of Lyndon Johnson voted for repeal of our Declaration of Independence . . . voted for scrapping the United States Constitution . . . voted for encouragement and support by the Federal government of racial agitators to instigate more riots . . .
   Our forty-two million Johnson camp followers . . . voted to condone and accept the gradual destruction of all moral principles . . .
   Forty-two million Americans voted for Communizing our nation . . . (A pamphlet, *The 27,000,000*)

The United States is an insane asylum run by its worst patients. (Robert Welch, in a recent speech).

The Birch theorists have singled out the U. S. State Department for especially violent attacks. "Communist headquarters in Washington . . ." they have called it, and judged its policies as sure signs of a conspiracy at work. The editors of the Society's magazine have described the war in Korea as one "which traitors in Washington quickly transformed into a very successful device for getting Americans killed, squandering American money, subjecting the United States to a humiliating defeat . . ." and have said that the war in Vietnam was, according to *American Opinion* correspondent Eric Butler, "deliberately produced through treachery in Washington."
   The Society's 1966 evaluation of the United States (in the July-August issue of its magazine) was that it was 60% to 80% under the influence and control of the Communist conspiracy.
   The United Nations fares even worse in the Birchers'

evaluation. Welch insists in his members' *Bulletin* almost every month that the UN was planned by the Communists, that it is controlled by the Communists, and that it was designed specifically to suit Communist purposes.

Birchite speakers on the lecture platform contribute other examples of the extremism of the Society's general thinking and line. National Council member Tom Anderson, for instance, told an audience in the South:

> We've got to take a stand against becoming a dictatorship. It's not the comrade I'm worried about, it's the liberal rat he is nesting with.
>
> If we have morality and courage we can destroy the diabolical conspiracy of communism. Every communist and every pro-communist ought to be arrested, deported and hung.

Speaking at Denver in March, 1966, Mrs. Julia Brown, a major lecturer under the banner of the Society's American Opinion Speakers Bureau, charged that President Johnson "has done more for Communism than any other President."

The Birchers, it should be noted, hold out very little hope for the "insane" who, according to Welch, are running things in the United States, since they view mental health programs as a deep-rooted Red plot.

"The Communists," wrote the editors of *American Opinion* in the 1965 "Scoreboard" (July-August issue), "in a very considerable number of states . . . have induced the legislatures to enact 'mental health' laws to facilitate the incarceration of troublesome Americans." Observers first became aware of this fiendish scheme, they reported, on October 1, 1962, "when, in obedience to the specific demands of the Communist Party, a gang under the direction of Nicholas Katzenbach kidnapped General Edwin A. Walker in Oxford, Miss. . . ."

This line had been taken in Welch's magazine seven months earlier by Revilo P. Oliver, the Birch Society's master of theory and invective from the time of its founding until his resignation in August, 1966. Oliver wrote that " 'mental health' prisons are being increasingly used for the kidnapping and mental, if not physical, murder of patriotic Americans."

Sanity and Revilo P. Oliver

For eight years, Revilo P. Oliver, a classics professor at the University of Illinois, rode the apogee of the Birch flight of mind. He magnified the terrors of the Far Right in triphammer prose, evoking from the Birch membership greater acclaim than any other Society spokesman. No innocent he, he was also no bystander. He was one of the founders of The John Birch Society, and he was a member of its ruling National Council. He was also the book reviewer for *American Opinion*.

It was Oliver who wrote the notorious "Marxmanship in Dallas," an article in Welch's magazine charging that one possible reason President Kennedy had been assassinated by Communist plotters was because he had been about to "turn American."

In a 1959 speech Oliver declared Cuba to be "an island largely populated by mongrels," and in a 1965 *American Opinion* article he found Washington, D.C., largely populated by "hordes of thieves, perverts, and traitors." In the same article he wrote:

> More than once, the directors of what calls itself the National Council of Churches have been caught in the very act of importing into the United States and escorting about the country identified agents of the Soviet Secret Police . . .

It is a lie, Oliver has written, that the Nazis killed 6,000,000 Jews. It is equally a lie, he has declared, that the races are equal. He wrote in 1964 that "the United States

110

is now engaged in an insane, but terribly effective, effort to destroy the American people and Western civilization by subsidizing, both at home and abroad, the breeding of the intellectually, physically, and morally unfit . . ."

It is hardly surprising that Oliver has been a student, and a teacher, of the conspiracy or "Devil" theory of man's history. "It is clear," he wrote in the December, 1964, issue of *American Opinion*, "that there is in the human species some biological strain of either atavism or degeneracy that manifests itself in a hatred of mankind and a lust for evil for its own sake."

Those exercising this lust for evil—"evil" being considered as the progress of humanity out of the Dark Ages—are the Great Conspirators, the secret directors of history. The whole view was spelled out for the twentieth century by an Englishwoman, the late Nesta H. Webster, in a racist and anti-Semitic book entitled *World Revolution—The Plot Against Civilization.* (A similar work by Mrs. Webster bore the title *Secret Societies and Subversive Movements*). The rambling, paranoid exegesis of Mrs. Webster, long a standard of the professional hatemongers, was favorably reviewed in the January, 1965, issue of *American Opinion* by Revilo P. Oliver, who found it "simply indispensable" to students of the conspiracy.

Oliver himself had collaborated with men who envisioned the most sinister aspects of the Great World Plot. He shared the platform at a Congress of Freedom convention (Shreveport, La., April 13-17, 1966) with two blatant anti-Semites, Ned Touchstone and Richard Cotten. He had once been a featured speaker at a convention of Soldiers of the Cross, the organization headed by Kenneth Goff, a former lieutenant of Gerald Smith. Goff has been a notorious anti-Semite for some two decades, and today is active in support of the Minutemen's Patriotic Party.

The effect of Oliver's conspiracy-hunting has been evident in the tone of the Birch Society's official propaganda line, which has become a massive assault against the twentieth century and against the fabric of American society itself.

In the 1965 *American Opinion* "Scoreboard," for example, it was stated that

> . . . progress in *every* field . . . is "progress" toward barbarism, *designed* to weaken and destroy our moral instincts and our capacity for self-respect—*designed,* in short, to kill loyalty to the United States, respect for the white race, comprehension of Western civilization, and veneration of God. The simultaneous movement in a hundred supposedly unrelated segments of our national life cannot be mere coincidence.

The editors of Welch's magazine wrote that they were "especially grateful to Associate Editor Revilo P. Oliver" for help with the evaluation of the United States partially quoted above.

Thus, for eight years did the thinking of The John Birch Society whirl in a strange, suspicion-loaded atmosphere created by the viewpoint and mentality that Revilo P. Oliver typifies. And Robert Welch himself referred to Oliver as "an authentic genius of the first water, *and quite possibly the world's greatest living scholar."*

Oliver's Resignation

On the Fourth of July weekend, 1966, however, Oliver electrified the audience at a mammoth Birchite rally in Boston with a speech replete with open and unmistakable anti-Semitism.

The occasion was the annual three-day "New England Rally for God, Family, and Country," an affair of which Col. Laurence Bunker, a member of the Birch Society's National Council, is chairman, and which is managed by top-level employees of the Society at its headquarters.

Actually, the Oliver speech was the last in a series of

events which soon drew to a dramatic climax. The chain of relevant events began in February, 1966—when the Anti-Defamation League issued a report charging that, among other dangerous trends, the Society also was contributing to anti-Semitism; the report documented instances of anti-Semitism in Birchite ranks.

Later that same month, an extraordinary organization was formed—the "Jewish Society of Americanists," founded by Jewish members of the Birch Society to offer sympathetic Jews a forum and to warn the Jewish community of the dangers of the "Communist conspiracy" (Birch version, of course). The JSA was openly a Birch Society affiliate from the start. Its spokesmen—chief among them, Samuel L. Blumenfeld, one of Robert Welch's top editors—made this clear. (At the beginning of 1967, the JSA had perhaps 250 members, including non-Jewish supporters.)

There were, during the next few months, persistent rumors in Birchite circles that certain JSA members had incipient misgivings about some aspects of the Birch atmosphere, specifically about certain anti-Semitic manifestations which they had seen documented in the ADL report.

Then came the heat of July, and the Revilo P. Oliver speech at Boston.

In his stentorian tones, Oliver told the audience of about 2,000 persons of the various hypotheses concerning the secret agency lurking behind the master conspiracy of the world—specifically naming the Communists, the "Illuminati," and the Jews. He gave clear credence to the existence of "a conspiracy of the Jews," citing what he called "satisfactory historical evidence" that this Jewish conspiracy was initiated back in the fifth century B.C.

More startling, however, to some ears was a passing remark in his torrent of words that day. He referred to a "beatific vision" on earth if "all the Jews were vaporized at dawn tomorrow . . ." The only trouble with it, he said, was that every educated man knew it just couldn't be so.

There were reports that, following the Oliver speech,

leaders of the Jewish Society of Americanists put pressure on Robert Welch and the Birch Society's executive committee to drop Oliver from the Society, that there were implied threats of resignation, and even rumblings about possible public denunciation of the Society for retaining a person objectionable to the Jews in its upper echelons.

It would appear that Welch found himself confronted with the necessity of making a choice: to drop Revilo P. Oliver and face a possible split in Society ranks, or to face the obvious public embarrassment of losing his much-vaunted little cabal of Jewish supporters, which served as useful and needed window-dressing to counteract the widespread impression that the Birch Society was not overly friendly to Jews and was therefore shunned by Jews.

The decision obviously was to be one based on expediency, rather than on principle—the question of Oliver's anti-Semitism itself. It was patently a public relations question: which course would least damage the Birch Society?

In August, Revilo P. Oliver resigned from the Birch Society, from its Council, and from his editorial position with Welch's magazine. At no time in the months that followed did the Society mention anti-Semitism as a factor in the resignation. Instead, it made every effort to depict the departure of Oliver (and of Slobodan Draskovich, another Council member who resigned at the same time, apparently in sympathy with Oliver) as merely the result of disagreement over policy and doctrine.

Nor did Robert Welch's organization repudiate Oliver, or even chide him. In fact, in the October, 1966, Birch *Bulletin*, Welch termed the Oliver and Draskovich resignations "regrettable."

The Davis Odyssey

While these things were happening in the spring and summer of 1966, a new and somewhat related thrust in the Birch Society's propaganda line developed, as Welch's public relations division spearheaded a major campaign against the Anti-Defamation League of B'nai B'rith. Reflecting a top-level policy decision of the Society, Thomas J. Davis, then its Eastern Regional Manager of Public Relations, undertook a nationwide speaking tour—his subject, "The Jewish Community and the John Birch Society." (Davis, as noted, resigned his paid position with the Society at the end of 1966 to go into private business.)

The Davis tour—from May, extending at least through November—proceeded from New York, New Haven, and Hartford in the East, and westward to Indianapolis, Fort Wayne and St. Louis, south to Oklahoma City, Houston, San Antonio, and Birmingham. Welch cheered for his spokesman in the August members' *Bulletin,* describing Davis's standard speech as well prepared and well received.

Davis reached for venomous words in his attacks. The ADL, praised by the last four Presidents of the United States, and by FBI Director J. Edgar Hoover—specifically praised, in Hoover's case, for its anti-Communist efforts—became in Davis's speeches a "Gestapo-type" organization and a "left-wing group" whose aim was to destroy "patriotic and anti-Communist groups in this country." Similar phrases had long been used by the most rabid anti-Semites in attacks on the ADL.

Davis also assailed a scholarly five-year study on "Christian Beliefs and Anti-Semitism" which had been sponsored by the ADL and undertaken by two distinguished sociologists under the auspices of the Research Survey Center of the University of California. A conference held in New York to discuss the findings of the study had received unreserved praise from Catholic, Presbyterian, Lutheran, Episcopalian, and Southern Baptist religious leaders. But Thomas J. Davis's distorted version of the study wholly misrepresented it as an attack on Christian church-going. Msgr. George C. Higgins, director of the Social Action Department of the National Catholic Welfare Conference, was compelled to write:

If the Birchites don't want to join in this struggle [against bigotry], so be it. But they have no business spreading false impressions about the Glock-Stark study.

Davis did not dispense entirely with the usual Birch techniques. He charged, of course, that the Anti-Defamation League advances the Communist cause, and added that the Birchers would expose the ADL because "like all Communist error it cannot stand exposure."

The ADL had released its report on the Birch Society only three months earlier, but it would be a mistake to consider Davis's coast-to-coast invective as mere rebuttal. In his long series of speeches Davis not only spoke *officially* for his organization, but echoed Founder Welch's prior pronouncements on anti-Semitism, the ADL, and the Communist overtones Welch claimed to see in both.

In 1965, Welch gave a three-day seminar for a small group at a private home in the Midwest. His whole presentation was recorded and the 22-hour monologue was then edited down to 18 hours and issued by the Society as *One Dozen Trumpets*—twelve record albums of four sides each. Price: $50.

At one point in his marathon seminar, Welch touched on the subject of anti-Semitism. He said in part:

Anti-Semitism has been the most powerful weapon the Communists have had at different times. In my opinion —I think you could prove it—anti-Semitism was created by the Communists for them to be able to use both sides . . .

In my opinion—and I don't know whether I'll leave this in this tape or not—maybe not—because I want to write a book about it—but the greatest creator of anti-Semitism in the United States for the last generation has been, of course, the Anti-Defamation League. Done more to create anti-Semitism, under the guise of stopping it and preventing it, than all other organizations put together. But what's more important—in my opinion—that's what it was founded for; that was its purpose—was to create

116

anti-Semitism. Just as so many things that the Communists have had a hand in behind the scenes are
created for the exact opposite of what they appear to
be created for. And the ADL has done an incredibly
good job of creating anti-Semitism . . .

The differences between the ADL and the Birch Society
were, in fact, far more fundamental than the unfounded
charges by Welch and Davis against an organization that
was fighting Communism long before Welch ever thought
of forming a radical group to save the country from the so-
called "Communist" threat posed, according to the Birchers,
by such Americans as Dwight Eisenhower, Earl Warren,
John Foster Dulles, and Allen Dulles.

The ADL has championed more democracy in the American republic; democracy, in the Birchite mythology is a
"fraud." The ADL has championed civil rights, equal
justice, and equal opportunity for all; civil rights, in the
Birchers' view is part of the great "conspiracy." In truth, it
was the whole democratic philosophy and tradition of the
ADL which made the Birch attack inevitable. It is, moreover, an immutable and automatic aspect of the Birch
Society "line" that all with whom it disagrees, and all
who disagree with it, who criticize it, or who merely hold
opposing views, are suspect—and none among the suspect
will long be spared the peculiar treatment the Society
reserves for "the enemy." And so the ADL found itself a
target of Birchite wrath—along with Presidents of the
United States, Cabinet members, judges, and others who
have served the nation well, and national organizations,
religious and secular, that have been bulwarks of the
American republic.

Welch and the Great Conspiracy

The activities and the writings of Revilo P. Oliver
remain relevant to any analysis of Birch Society thinking.
Oliver helped to direct the Society—and perhaps even

epitomized it—over a period of eight years from that day in Indianapolis when he, along with ten other men, helped Robert Welch to establish the organization. This man so highly acclaimed by Welch did much to set the ideological tone of The John Birch Society. He was certainly not repudiated and his teachings over the years had been well absorbed by many Birchers—including Founder Welch himself. Throughout his long association with Oliver, Robert Welch had expressed admiration for some of the professor's nightmare theories. Only three months after Oliver's resignation, the founder, president, and ideological leader of the Birch monolith adopted as his own some of the favored fantasies of the Oliver-Nesta Webster cult.

Welch wrote a 30-page tract entitled *The Truth in Time,* which initially appeared as the lead article in the November, 1966, issue of *American Opinion.* He described it as "an outline of the gradual integration of evil forces into what has now become the Communist conspiracy, from its amorphous beginnings in the Eighteenth Century up to its present worldwide reach with tentacles of steel."

The tract presents the thesis that in the eighteenth century a group of secret societies—foremost among them the "Illuminati," founded in 1776 by one Adam Weishaupt in Bavaria—had conspired to overthrow "all existing human institutions" and become "the all-powerful rulers of a 'new order' of civilization." The first overt action of the plotters, Welch declares, was the French Revolution, and the first open declaration of their purpose the Communist *Manifesto* of Karl Marx.

But, writes Welch, "the Communist movement is only a tool of the total conspiracy. As secret as the Communist activities and organizations generally appear, they are part of an open book compared to the secrecy enveloping some higher degree of this diabolic force."

Illuminati, secrecy, tentacles, diabolic force—such are the terms found in the output of Nesta Webster and of Revilo Oliver. Welch has termed these secret, super-Communist

118

plotters "the INSIDERS"—a useful term because it is vague
—sufficiently vague to allow each loyal reader to insert his
own cast of diabolical characters.

"By 1914," Welch writes, "the INSIDERS, with comparatively few agents but tremendous influence and cun-
ning," had brought about in the United States such
elements of the grand plot as the personal income tax
and the direct election of Senators (democracy is "the worst
of all forms of government"), as well as the Federal Reserve
System—this last, a favorite whipping-boy of the professional anti-Semites, though Welch did not mention a "Jewish conspiracy" as having played any such role.

After the INSIDER-created World War I, Welch continues, the "world conspiracy" becomes identified almost
totally with the rise of Communism, its takeover in Russia,
its conquest of Europe by means of the INSIDER-created
World War II. (In the Birch Society production, *One
Dozen Trumpets,* Welch declared that the Communists had
"goaded the unsuspecting Hitler into attacking Poland.")

Welch's post-war analysis runs the all-too-familiar Birch
course from "traitorous influences within our own government" to the point where today, in Vietnam, "we are commanded by our enemies."

A Conservative Awakening?

Late in 1965, a few American conservatives—among them
William F. Buckley, Jr., editor of *National Review*—blind
for so long, and doggedly so—began to catch glimpses of the
fact that many if not all Birchers live in the same fantasy
world as does Mr. Welch and that they are not merely
misled conservatives following a misguided leader.

Though Buckley and the others had been slow to realize
it, the relationship between leader and followers in the
Birch monolith had been best described by Welch himself in the *Blue Book* seven years earlier:

The men who join the John Birch Society during the

next few months or few years are going to do so primarily because they believe in me and what I am doing and are willing to accept my leadership anyway.

Buckley originally had believed, nonetheless, that Birchers could be separated from their leader in an overall view; now all that had changed. In a special six-part section of the October 19, 1965, issue of *National Review*, Buckley and his editors—including James Burnham and Frank S. Meyer—announced that they now believed the Birch Society to represent a threat to the conservative movement—and that it did so because Birch members appeared to believe and support the Welchian conspiracy mythology. The *National Review* editors had also discovered that this mythology had become "more virulent," and that there had been no effective movement from within the Society "to contain Mr. Welch's utterances, or to remove him as the Society's leader." Editor Meyer, writing on "The Birch Malady," concluded:

> It is no longer possible to consider the Society merely as moving towards legitimate objectives in a misguided way. However worthy the original motivations of those who have joined it and who apologize for it, it is time for them to recognize that the John Birch Society is rapidly losing whatever it had in common with patriotism or conservatism—and to do so before their own minds become warped by adherence to its unrolling psychosis of conspiracy.

Meyer also paused to deal with the Birch line on the civil rights movement as part of a Communist plot. He wrote:

> It is true that here (as everywhere it profits them) Communist groups are active, seeking to take advantage of the turmoil, and are sometimes successful in penetrating sections of the leadership of the movement. But the movement is not a Communist movement, as the John

Birch Society implies with every device of rhetoric, with pictures, with innuendo, and often with straight-forward statement.

(Meyer echoed the words of J. Edgar Hoover, who had stated: ". . . The American civil rights movement is not, and never has been dominated by the Communists—because the overwhelming majority of civil rights leaders in this country, both Negro and white, have recognized and rejected Communism as a menace to the freedom of all.")

The Birch Line on Vietnam

If the Buckley awakening, and the developing split between his followers and the purveyors of Welch's "surrealisms" and "paranoid and unpatriotic drivel" (Buckley), had revolved about the Birchers' conspiratorial propaganda line, it seemed to center on the question of Vietnam—and Welch's very peculiar views about it. Buckley's point was made in a *National Review* article by James Burnham.

The Birch Society, Burnham wrote, was "lined up with its supposedly diametric opposite, the Left, in support of getting out." He concluded that the Birchers' Vietnam position "confirms, not for the first time, that any American who seriously wants to contribute to his country's security and well-being and to oppose Communism will have to stay clear of the JBS."

Burnham's attack stemmed from Welch's exposition of the Society's Vietnam policy which had been spelled out only a few months earlier in the August, 1965, *Bulletin*. In it, Welch in effect advocated a "Get US out!" policy with respect to Vietnam. He based this position on his firm conviction that the Communists were calling the shots on both sides of the Vietnam conflict and that the aim of the Communists—in Hanoi and in Washington—was to damage United States prestige abroad and to enable the Johnson administration to complete the fastening of

121

police state controls on the American domestic scene, using a wartime situation as a smokescreen and as an excuse. In the August, 1965, *Bulletin,* Welch wrote:

> Does anybody doubt that we could have wiped the North Vietnam Communists out of South Vietnam within three months, at any time during the past several years, and made them glad to stay out, if we had really wanted to do so? . . . Does anybody think that there has been any lessening of the power or ruthlessness of the Communist influences in Washington since 1953?

He went on to explain how this Communist influence works:

> What on earth is the matter with our compatriots in the American anti-Communist movement, anyway? The Communists, by exercising a minimum of discipline and of control by propaganda, over a relatively few thousand beatniks and halfbaked collegiate brats, and by passing the word to a few of their highly placed agents, create a leftwing demand that the United States pull out of Vietnam! And this gambit fools the American people into thinking that we are serving some purpose, other than exactly what the Communists want, by what we are doing in Vietnam! Naturally, the Communists have been doing everything they could to advance the theme that it is our patriotic and humanitarian duty to "stand firm" in Vietnam, and to keep on increasing our forces and our involvement there as the war is "escalated"—exactly according to their plans—into a greater Korea. What on earth would you expect? For twenty years we have been taken steadily down the road to Communism by steps supposedly designed, and always sold to the American people, *as a means of opposing Communism.* Will we never learn anything from experience?

Welch saw the war in Vietnam as a diversionary tactic, and warned:

> . . . In the long run, you are going to see the fact that we are at war used increasingly, and ever more brazenly,

to enable the Communists in government, in the press, in the pulpit, and in every other division of our national life, to label all criticism of their captive Administration as treasonous. You will see that Administration begin to establish controls over the lives and actions of the American people which will make all the regimentation we have had so far look like a study in free enterprise; and begin suppressing all opposition by the usual Communist police-state methods.

At that time, Welch declared that the most desirable way of carrying out his exhortation that the U.S. get out of Vietnam would be by "winning the war quickly and completely." But he added that he would "stake our reputation for fifteen years of 'calling the shots' correctly on there being less chance of this Administration conducting an honest war in Vietnam, for honestly anti-Communist purposes, than there is of Khrushchev being elected president of the United States Chamber of Commerce."
Welch added:

. . . A few of our members have become disturbed because our slogan with regard to the United Nations, Get US out! is being taken by some to mean 'Get US out of Vietnam!' And if it becomes desirable to avoid that confusion, we can change the usual form of the message to: 'Get US out of the UN!' But it may soon become clear that there is little difference in the effective meaning of either version . . .

So we say Get US out!, and add no ifs or buts. From the very time the slogan was first conceived, we have recognized the possibility that there might be those in due course who would interpret it broadly, as follows: "Get us out of this whole foreign worldwide mess in which we are playing so cruel and so ignominious a part, and let's clean up all of the crime and dirtiness, and deficits and moral debauchery here at home.' But we have no objection to this meaning. We still . . . say, as emphatically as we can: Get US out! And we should like to repeat, for emphasis, that we knew exactly what we were saying and were looking ahead to this kind of situation, when we first coined the phrase: *Get US out!*

In the wake of the *National Review* attack on his August, 1965, position, and in the face of continuing concern by his members about it, Welch began to shift his emphasis with respect to Vietnam. The slogan "Get US out!" was replaced in December, 1965, by a new battle cry—"When do we win this war in Vietnam—and why not?"

This posture had a tougher ring to it—while not really saying anything meaningful, unless one focuses on the barbed hook at the end, with its implications that there were hidden reasons for the fact that the United States had not yet won a quick and overwhelming victory in Vietnam. The "why not" was a clearly telegraphed signal to Birchers across the country that the Communist conspiracy in Washington was preventing a quick and decisive victory, and by taking a seemingly "hawklike" position instead of sounding like a neo-isolationist, Welch also made it slightly harder for his critics to draw the obvious comparisons with the cries of Radical Leftists for a U.S. withdrawal from Vietnam.

At the same time, The John Birch Society *Bulletin* characterized the Vietnam war as being run by the Southeast Asia Treaty Organization (SEATO). Welch linked SEATO to the United Nations, as further evidence that the war against Hanoi was also being run by Communists since the Birch line sees the UN as Communist-controlled. Welch said: "We are sending our men to fight in a war against the Communists, which war is actually being run by the Communists." In the June 1966, *Bulletin,* apparently to vindicate his original position, he wrote:

> *Because of the war in Vietnam*—in order that we may have any chance to win it and *then* bring our boys home —Get US out! of the United Nations.

At the end of 1966, Welch came up with yet another version of his dovelike-hawklike slogan on Vietnam. This time it was "Let's win this war in Vietnam—and get out!"

Yet another battle cry, also set forth as a question and also designed to camouflage Welch's basic neo-isolationism, emerged at about the same time: "Why fight 'em in Vietnam and help 'em everywhere else?"

Early in 1967, Welch made it clear that the Vietnam issue would be a major concern of the Birch Society during the year. In the February, 1967, *Bulletin,* he announced that all his speeches in the weeks ahead would be devoted exclusively to the war in Vietnam. Accompanying the *Bulletin* was a 20-page pamphlet outlining the Society's position on the war which Welch had hammered out so painfully during a period of more than a year. The pamphlet was called *The Truth About Vietnam* and was designed as the basic document in the new propaganda offensive, just as *Two Revolutions at Once* had laid down the Birchite line for the war against the civil rights movement. And *The Truth About Vietnam* projected yet another Welchian slogan on the war: "Victory, Then Peace!"

Whatever fine distinctions and differentiations Welch has made—off-again, on-again—sometimes urging U.S. withdrawal from Vietnam, sometimes raising insinuating questions—the basic theme of his comments has always been predictable. No matter how it has been sliced, it has always been the Welchian "conspiracy" syndrome—Communists everywhere, Communists "calling the shots" in Washington, as well as in Moscow, Peking and Hanoi, the American nation being sold out and betrayed by its own leaders who are invariably evil men in high places.

Welch's charges of treason and betrayal leveled at American administrations, past and present, Republican and Democratic, give rise to interesting speculation about his own self-proclaimed patriotism and the patriotism of those who follow him in The John Birch Society. For Welch himself has developed an interesting theory of analysis about Communist propaganda and Communist dogma. It is called the "principle of reversal" which, Welch contends, the Communists employ to deceive and confuse their opponents. As a result of this tactic, Welch argues, things are not always what they seem and the Communists often publicly oppose that which they favor, and favor that which they oppose. If the Communists want a UN Secretary General retained, Welch argues, they agitate for his removal. This forces the United States to stand firm for his retention—which is, of course, exactly what the Reds want.

The principle of reversal is a handy tool for Welch. If the Communists stick to form, there is no problem. But if they take a certain position that does not conform to Welchian expectation, that unexpected twist in the Red line is explained away by the founder as an example of the principle of reversal in operation.

The bizarre conclusions that can be drawn from the use of Welch's principle of reversal and from the conspiracy theory of history become clear when they are applied to Welch himself and to his Birch Society.

If one—hypothetically, of course—applies the principle of reversal to their self-proclaimed anti-Communist propaganda and activities, one might conclude that Welch and the Society are thereby masking their own pro-Communism.

And if one—hypothetically, of course—applies a conspiracy theory of history to the activities of Welch and his organization, one might raise these questions:

If a man weakens the faith of his countrymen in their national leaders and their great national institutions by implying treason and Communism among them . . .

And if a man charges that one recent American President was a "dedicated, conscious agent of the Communist conspiracy" and that other Presidents have also served the Communist cause . . .

If a man publishes accusations that the highest court in the land serves the Communist cause in decisions it renders . . .

Or if a man charges that American soldiers in the field

126

are "commanded by their enemies" in Washington . . .

And if he charges that officials in Washington are sending the sons and husbands and brothers of American women to fight a war in Southeast Asia as a way of speeding the subjugation of the United States to a police-state dictatorship . . .

If, in sum, a man thus plays upon the fears and the worries and the anxieties of his countrymen for admittedly political purposes, could he not be viewed as undermining his country's strength and unity, and as serving the Communist cause himself?

These are, of course, only hypothetical notions, but the principle of reversal and the conspiracy theory of history lead to bizarre conclusions—none more bizarre than those reached by Founder Welch in handing down the ideological program of The John Birch Society.

CHAPTER TEN

The
Birchers and
Anti-Semitism

Thomas J. Davis's attempts to ridicule the Anti-Defamation League charges concerning instances of anti-Semitism in The John Birch Society—and to answer such charges merely by adding the ADL to a growing list of those seen as "Communist" in the Society's eyes—has not explained the fact that The John Birch Society has had a continuing problem with anti-Semites attracted to its fold. Nor have Davis's speeches explained why the Society has had so little success in dealing with the problem—if, indeed, anything more than token attempts have been made in this direction.

Admitting in *Bulletins* to his members that which he has denied publicly, Robert Welch has found it necessary on several occasions to warn against anti-Semites in his ranks. With typical Birchite perversity, of course, he has mixed such warnings with "principle of reversal" slaps at the critics who correctly diagnosed his problem. As in the November, 1965, *Bulletin,* for example, when he wrote:

> Let's suppose you happen to believe, for instance, that the Anti-Defamation League, always under the guise of protecting the Jews from anti-Semitism—and certainly with that intention on the part of many of its leaders—has actually done more to cause and promote anti-Semitism than any other group or force in America. Suppose you even go further—as do some of my Jewish friends—

and believe that the ADL was originally designed by Communists for that very purpose . . . then why on earth help them, and the Communists behind them, to carry out this nefarious scheme, by yourself reacting in exactly the way the Communists have planned and wanted?

In the same *Bulletin,* Welch propounded an astounding doctrine, carrying the conspiracy theory to hitherto unplumbed depths:

> . . . there came a period of some forty years when an abnormal percentage of the visible leadership of the Communist Conspiracy was of Jewish ancestry . . . And these traitors to their race—as well as to all mankind—worked and schemed and plotted to have themselves hated, *not as Communists, but as Jews.*

But that Welch could imagine so fiendish a conspiracy is hardly surprising after one has read the sentence quoted above concerning "Jewish ancestry"—an echo of the oldest anti-Semitic canards.

The Society's trouble with anti-Semites is illustrated by the cases of Californians Richard Cotten and James Oviatt. Cotten, a radio propagandist who preaches that Communism was financed by "those people" in New York and that the U.S. State Department is run by Jews, gathered adherents from among Birch Society members in the Far West—to whom he recommended the publications of such hate mongers as Gerald Smith, Don Bell, and the late Conde McGinley. He thus became a major cause of controversy and dissension within Welch's organization. The trouble became so acute by the spring of 1965 that Welch sent to every chapter leader in the United States a special, printed memorandum warning Birchers away from Cotten and his teachings. It was Cotten's fondness for armed "anti-Communism" (such as that of the Minutemen) and for a certain Korean writer Welch considered pro-Red, more than his blatant anti-Semitism, that aroused Welch's ire.

James Oviatt, a Los Angeles haberdasher who had been a member of the Society, was a patron of Wesley Swift, a notorious anti-Semite. Oviatt mailed to his store's clients packets of hate literature including material based on the classic fraud of anti-Semitica, *The Protocols of the Learned Elders of Zion.* Oviatt was dropped by Welch from membership after the Anti-Defamation League made his activities public. In August, 1965, William F. Buckley, Jr., published a letter he had received from Oviatt after a previous Buckley blast against Welch and his Society's extremism. Oviatt wrote:

> I am just wondering what Zionist Jew wrote this article? Could it have been Lippmann, or Goldberg, or even Abe—Johnson's attorney? . . . I have known Bob Welch for over 15 years. I think he told the truth about Eisenhower.

At about the time of its exposé of Oviatt, the ADL published an analysis of the anti-Semitism in articles written for Welch's magazine by Westbrook Pegler. Welch wrote the League: "We were already becoming unhappy ourselves with some of the attitudes in Mr. Pegler's writings."

In the meantime, *American Opinion* had dropped Pegler, who went on to grace the platform of Gerald Smith. Late in 1965, he began writing a column for *The Councilor,* the racist, anti-Semitic organ of the Louisiana White Citizens' Councils. It is worthy of note, however, that while Welch dropped Oviatt and Pegler, a Boston woman who has made financial contributions to Smith's anti-Jewish "Christian Nationalist Crusade," Olive Simes, has been listed as a stockholder in *American Opinion* magazine.

The Anti-Semitic Background

The appearance of such persons on the Birch scene are not isolated incidents—nor are they especially surprising. Welch and his Society have a lack of alertness—a kind of blind spot—about the activities in which such people have been engaged, even when such activities have been carefully made a matter of public knowledge.

As early as 1952, Welch cited a pamphlet by Joseph Kamp as source material for his book, *May God Forgive Us.* (Kamp is the long-time extremist pamphleteer whose writings have been filled with ill-concealed anti-Semitic innuendo, and who is now identified with Liberty Lobby.) Later, Welch paid Kamp $100 to check the manuscript of his 1954 book, *The Life of John Birch.* Still later, sections of Welch's infamous book on Eisenhower, *The Politician,* appeared to have been taken almost verbatim from the March 15, 1952, issue of Kamp's *Headlines.* (Welch later wrote he had not been aware that many considered Kamp to be an extremist pamphleteer and declared he would never allow the Birch Society to become a haven for anti-Semites so long as he was at its helm).

In *The Politician,* Lucille Miller of Bethel, Vt., was described by Welch as "a patriotic but not too cautious Vermont woman." Actually, she was a blatant anti-Semite, and had been so identified quite publicly.

Still another authority cited by Welch in *The Politician* —sometimes referred to as his "Black Book"—was Merwin Hart, who had been one of America's most prolific voices of anti-Semitism through almost three decades.

Hart, who died in 1962, had been active in Coughlinite and isolationist causes during the pre-World War II days. His association with Robert Welch first came to public view in 1959, when he was listed on the advisory board of the first Birch Society front group, the "Committee Against Summit Entanglements." Later, Hart appeared in the Birch apparatus as a Society chapter leader. At least two supporters of Hart's National Economic Council have served as members of the National Council of the Birch Society.

In spite of Welch's periodic admonitions, the tendency of The John Birch Society to attract anti-Semites has persisted, and plagues the organization. Welch had recognized

131

the problem as early as 1963, when he issued a pamphlet called *The Neutralizers,* criticizing and warning against those who "neutralized" the Birch Society's program with fits of irrelevant anti-Semitism or with "tangentitis" (fanatical support for Right Wing causes other than those canonized by the Society itself).

The pamphlet assailed some of the fundamental tenets of the Jew-haters and singled out bigot Wesley Swift and the "British-Israel" cult of Anglo-Saxon racism for criticism. It did not mention Merwin Hart or Joe Kamp. What is perhaps most significant in *The Neutralizers* is the fact that Welch found it necessary to devote 16 pages to the task of proving to the membership of his Society that Communism is *not* a Jewish conspiracy.

The Anti-Semitic Foreground

The attraction of anti-Semites to The John Birch Society has not gone unnoticed. As pointed out earlier, the Society made wide and exhaustive use of the report of the first investigation of the Society by California's Senate Fact-Finding Sub-Committee on Un-American Activities in 1963, although understandably saying little or nothing about a more recent report by the same body in June, 1965. The 1965 report found "an influx of emotionally unstable people" into the Society and a "dangerous increase of anti-Semitism among a minority of membership."

Rousselot was quoted at that time by the Associated Press as explaining: "We have been concerned with the problem of anti-Semitic infiltrators." (By thus labeling anti-Semites as outside "infiltrators," he apparently sought to avoid what is actually an inherent problem of the Society and to dodge its implications.) Rousselot added: "We have dealt very decisively with the problem."

Just how "decisively" has the Birch Society dealt with the problem? Recent history suggests an answer . . .

Item: As mentioned previously, on the July 4th weekend,

1966, in Boston, Revilo P. Oliver delivered a blatantly anti-Semitic speech in front of a crowd of 2,000—which included Robert Welch and several high officials of the Birch Society. A few weeks later, Oliver resigned his positions in the Society because *he* could not "in conscience" remain. The anti-Semitism of Oliver, a Birch founder, Council member, and editor, and one of the Society's leading theoreticians for eight years, has never been repudiated or publicly criticized.

Item: A speaker before a Birch-front TACT committee meeting in Azusa, Calif., on October 11, 1966, declared: "Anyone who does not subscribe to the Son of God being our savior is a sinner and a Communist." He added: "This is a Christian nation with a Christian heritage, and any other group is subversive."

Item: Something very nearly approaching the "real name" gimmick, a standard device of anti-Semites, appeared in the July-August, 1966, issue of Welch's *American Opinion*. On page 69, an introductory article to the "Scoreboard" states: "Bronstein (alias Trotsky) boasted that he captured the centralized government of Russia with a force of just one thousand disciplined revolutionaries, many of whom he had trained in New York."

When there is another mention of Trotsky on page 69, he is not even called "Trotsky," but this time merely "Bronstein."

The use of an obviously identifiable Jewish surname serves no discernible purpose here but to point to a person's being Jewish. What further intent may be present in the writer's mind can only be surmised. *American Opinion* uses the device even more startlingly in another place (page 70) in the same article, where a lengthy sentence ends with these words: ". . . and Finklestein (alias Litvinov), would be punished, not with proper execution, but with only a mild and temporary exile."

The Universal Jewish Encyclopedia gives Litvinov's family name as "Wallach." It is given as "Finklestein," however, in Fritsch's *Handbook on the Jewish Question,* which once was the bible of anti-Semitism in Nazi Germany.

Item: The April 27, 1966, issue of the Birch Society publication, *Review of the News,* referring to left-oriented writer I. F. Stone, described something "which obviously made Stone (Isidor Feinstein) blink."

Item: A pamphlet by Joseph P. Kamp attacking Jewish leaders has been sold at the literature counters at the rallies "For God, Family, and Country," the annual Birchite affair at which Revilo P. Oliver delivered his anti-Semitic remarks in 1966.

Item: The Detroit *Free Press* reported early in 1966 that Chris Panos, a Birch Society chapter leader, had handed out anti-Semitic tracts to trusted chapter members. He was quoted as stating: "I'm not saying it at chapter meetings, but anyone who knows the truth about it knows the Jews are behind the Communists and the niggers. The Jews go talking about six million being killed by Hitler. There weren't that many. And why weren't any big Jews killed?"

Item: In 1965, a letter was circulated in Farmland, Ind., attacking the Anti-Defamation League as "a secret police . . . [an] atom-powered Communist front." The letter openly described this as a quote from a leaflet by Maj. Robert H. Williams, a notorious anti-Semite.

Item: In a 1966 report on The John Birch Society, the ADL pointed out that Nesta H. Webster's anti-Jewish books—*World Revolution—The Plot Against Civilization* and *Secret Societies and Subversive Movements*—were being sold in several Society bookstores. The Society did not immediately withdraw the books from sale—as it did the works of anti-Semites Marilyn Allen, Kenneth Goff, and Richard Cotten from other stores after the ADL had reported their availability. Instead, the Webster books which in part discussed a conspiratorial Jewish power lurking behind Communism, were for a time included by Robert Welch in the official, recommended "book list" of

The John Birch Society. Early in 1967, they were dropped from a later and revised book list.

The Silent (?) Butler

Early in 1965, the name of Eric Butler began to appear in the pages of *American Opinion*. This was the new Far East correspondent for Welch's magazine. And this marked the end of the myth that anti-Semitism existed only on the fringes, on the lower, less controllable levels of the Birch domain.

Eric Butler had been recognized for over a quarter of a century as one of Australia's leading anti-Semites. Back in 1947, Butler wrote in his own publication, the *New Times*:

> Ever since their active participation in the crucifixion of Christ, the Jewish leaders have worked ceaselessly to undermine and destroy the Christian faith. They have always believed and still believe . . . that the Jewish leaders are destined to rule the world.

In that same year, Butler wrote a 166-page book, *The International Jew—The Truth About the Protocols of Zion,* which a spokesman for the Catholic archdiocese in Sydney called an "exhibition of anti-Semitism at its worst . . . a disgraceful and mischievous production which is calculated to do harm to its readers . . ."

Eric Butler's views changed little through the years. A *New Times* editorial on June 16, 1962, spoke of "the vital role played by Jews in the Communist espionage systems." Earlier, on September 12, 1958, a more personal insult: "What is meant by the word gentleman does not exist among Jews. The genuine Jew fails in this innate good breeding . . ."

Butler came to the United States in January, 1964. On the 19th of that month he addressed a meeting in Los Angeles held under the chairmanship of Gerald Smith,

America's most notorious anti-Jewish propagandist. Later that spring, Butler toured Canada under the sponsorship of Ron Gostick, publisher of the anti-Semitic *Canadian Intelligence Service.*

In April, 1965, Eric Butler's first article in *American Opinion* appeared. His reports as the magazine's official Far East correspondent were published regularly thereafter. In the 1965 "Scoreboard" issue—wherein "Communist" influence in each nation of the world is annually estimated by Birch standards—Butler was assigned, ironically, to cover the area of Arab-Israel tensions. On Israel he reported: "This country's politics must be assessed against its pro-Communist background"—an astounding denial of historic fact which itself ought, perhaps, to be "assessed" against the author's own background.

"Eric D. Butler," his biographical sketch in Welch's magazine reads, "is National Director of the League of Rights, Australia's most significant anti-Communist organization." Actually, the League of Rights, founded by Butler some years earlier, is an organized anti-Semitic group of some significance.

In October, 1965, a report made at a synod of the Australian Anglican Church by its vicar, the Rev. D. J. Pope, declared that an anti-Semitic group was engaged in secret infiltration of the churches. The report further charged that the group was spreading the lie "that the Jews are trying to seize control of the world," and that it was "reviving old techniques used against the Jews." The vicar's report identified the infiltrating group as the League of Rights—the organization founded and headed by The John Birch Society's Far East "expert."

In February, 1966, the Anti-Defamation League called public attention to Eric Butler's background. Birch Society officials Welch and Rousselot suggested there would be some kind of investigation of the charges in the ADL report. Three months later, however, Butler's by-line still appeared in the Society's magazine; this was in May, the month during which Thomas J. Davis began his nationwide assault on the ADL, labeling the report of anti-Semitism problems within Birch ranks as a "smear."

The Welch-Rousselot-Davis reactions merely underlined the basic point of the ADL report. Again, the Birch Society attacked its critics rather than its critical problem.

And, interestingly, the Society continued to claim expert knowledge of the worldwide activities of secret conspirators —while pleading ignorance of the most public and publicized activities of its own man in Australia. Within a short while, however, Butler's name had disappeared from the *American Opinion* table of contents, though there was talk around Birch headquarters during the summer of 1966 that Butler had prepared the "Scoreboard" notes for the July-August issue anonymously. It was noted also that in subsequent issues of Welch's magazine, the only area "Reports" published without a by-line were those dealing with the Far East. There was, about the whole Eric Butler affair—in contrast to the noise of the Davis tour—a noticeable silence.

CHAPTER ELEVEN

The John Birch Society and Politics

The ultimate goal of The John Birch Society is political power.

Robert Welch's continual protestations that his is a "nonpolitical" organization are belied by his own words and by the deeds of his followers in the years since 1958 when, at the founding of the Society, Welch made clear that its aim was to achieve an eventual political victory for Right Wing thought. His words at that time are preserved in the *Blue Book* of the Society.

> We are at a stage, gentlemen, where the only sure political victories are achieved by non-political organizations; by organization which has . . . a backbone, and cohesiveness, and strength, and definiteness of direction, which are impossible for the old-style political party organization . . .
>
> . . . Nobody knows, and there is no way of finding out, how many millions of dollars Reuther spent in the last election, or how many tens of thousands of precinct workers he was able to put on the job. But with a million men and the resources consistent with the dedication of those men which we are presupposing, we could move in on the elections thereafter with both more manpower and more resources than Reuther will be able to marshal by that time. (pp. 111-112)

. . . We shall have to use politicians, support politicians, create politicians, and help the best ones we can find get elected. (p. 121)

Finally, and probably most important of all these courses of action, we would put our weight into the political scales in this country just as fast and as far as we could. For unless we can eventually, and in time, reverse by political action the gradual surrender of the United States to Communism, the ultimate alternative of reversal by military uprising is fearful to contemplate. (p. 110)

Founded on this obviously political note, The John Birch Society has launched a campaign admittedly to "control the political action" in a majority of the Congressional districts throughout the United States. By urging Society members to become politically "active," and by involving itself openly in activities on purely political issues—including specific items of legislation—Welch's organization hopes to effect a total change in the political thinking of the American people. The statement made at various times by Welch himself, by the Society's public relations director, John Rousselot, and by other top Society officials, that "the John Birch Society is not a political organization," is contradicted by many pages of official Birch doctrine.

In the *Blue Book* (p. 127) Welch says of the Society's dedication to "less government and more responsibility" (emphasis added):

"An honest adherence to that principle and those directions . . . will settle in the minds of our followers and ourselves almost all questions which may arise, *concerning either candidates or issues, in the field of political effort.* And yet it is broad enough, I believe, to be comprehensive with regard to all that we really desire to attain *through political action.*"

And summing up the Society's proposed "educational" program, he says (p. 142):

There, gentlemen, is our arguement, or that part of it

which applies, as I think it should be used *in the political field primarily for political purposes."*

The work to be undertaken by Mr. Welch's followers, which is described as including the luring of non-Birchers into Society activities, is again (p. 162) phrased in political terms:

"In the political arena, we shall try to make the word Americanism useful as a constructive opposite of Communism, and attract to our support many Americanists who may not be members of our Society . . ."

And in an exhortation to his members, Welch employed the term "nonpolitical" in a paradoxical if not hypocritical context (page 3 of the November, 1964, members' *Bulletin*):

"It was and is necessary to have Conservative candidates fully and widely backed by the labors of such a continuing non-political organization, to parallel and match the decisive help now given Liberal candidates by Walter Reuther's COPE, before Conservatives in general can win enough elections. The John Birch Society needs to be five times its present size for its members, even with all of their zeal and dedication, to fill this need. So come on in and help us."

The Political Crash Program

The "zeal and dedication" of Birch Society members, thus aroused, was soon channeled politically with Welch's proposal, first made in March, 1965, of a program of direct action. Outlined originally as part of a not-too-successful fund-raising drive aimed at raising about $18,000,000 over a two-year period, the crash program became an on-going project of the Birch Society, and one which clearly demonstrates the political mobilization of its members and their philosophy.

The project's aim, beyond 1965-66 fund-raising goals, was the placement of 1,000 Birch members (50 chapters) in each of 325 Congressional Districts to act as "ideological salesmen" to help elect "conservative" candidates. The aim was nothing less than changing the political complexion of the United States Congress by mobilizing Birch power at the local level. Robert Welch spelled it out in his initial appeal, called *Looking Ahead*:

> There are 435 Congressional Districts in the United States. Except in extremely rare instances and under the most unusual circumstances, there is no doubt that one hundred chapters of The John Birch Society, in any Congressional District, can exercise enough influence over political thinking within that district to control the political action there. And this would be done, without the Society itself ever endorsing a candidate, or taking any direct action in politics; but simply by our members proceeding on their own initiative from the basic principles and purposes of the Society, and persuading others to do the same . . .
>
> As a practical matter, therefore, let's consider what we could do with 50 chapters per district in 75% of the Congressional Districts in the whole United States . . . Now our chapters average about twenty members each. This means that we are talking about a working force of one thousand members for each Congressional District . . .
>
> Think of your own Congressional District and imagine one thousand truly informed and deeply dedicated neighborhood, community, and regional leaders, ceaselessly at work—nights as well as days, and weekends as well as nights—to inform and convince their fellow citizens.

One enterprise launched by the Society during 1966 seemed tailored to carry out Welch's grand design for influencing political action and electing Rightist candidates to office—goals he outlined at the founding meeting of the Birch organization, and again in *Looking Ahead*. Named "Project Knowledge," the program sought to reactivate former Birch members, to recruit new ones, and at the minimum to enlist non-Birchers in a Society-directed en-

141

deavor. To do so, the project was tied directly to the Birch-front TACT committees, which have been spearheading the Society's campaign against the civil rights movement and fanning the flames of the white backlash.

But "Project Knowledge" has a distinctly political twist and, in fact, seems to be conceived as a long-range program for political education and political action. It has been set up on a precinct basis, with activists and prospective members organized geographically along political boundary lines.

The ultimate goal is to lay the propaganda and organizational basis for eventual acceptance by the voters of Far Rightist political candidates throughout the country. The project itself, however, was launched on a pilot basis in several western states.

Project Knowledge appears to be Welch's answer to the AFL-CIO Committee on Political Education (COPE). It recalls the founder's proposal, eight years earlier, to "move in on the elections with both more manpower and more resources than Reuther will be able to marshal . . ."

What is more, Project Knowledge dovetails nicely with the openly political goals of the heavily Birchite *1976 Committee* and will, if successful, complement that group's ten-year crusade to save the Republic from the Communist conspiracy with Ezra Benson and Strom Thurmond as the 1968 standard-bearers.

Thus, the Birch Society—like the Communist Party in its grand design for achieving political power—spreads its message to build an active, indoctrinated cadre. When the cadre is built, and as it keeps growing, the process of infiltration and penetration into the vital organs of society begins to take place. Sometimes candidates are nominated, and a few even elected. But the cadre does not really expect at first to win many contests at the polls. Political activity is a vehicle for propaganda and recruitment, and an instrument for building the movement to larger proportions.

There is little doubt that when Robert Welch founded the Birch Society in 1958, he believed he would have no great problem in enlisting a million members in due course. By the beginning of 1967 he was still struggling below the 100,000 mark, and setting his sights on a more modest goal of 400,000. But the failure in numbers should blind no one to the ultimate *political* goal of the Society. In this struggle, the Birch Society has not yet given up.

In the Birch Society's penetration of American society, the single most important step has been the infiltration of the Republican Party by Welch's dedicated and indoctrinated cadres.

The ordeal of the Republican Party in its struggle with the intrusion of extremism in its ranks has been a matter of public record since the 1964 GOP convention at the Cow Palace in San Francisco. The problem existed when the delegates convened. (The Birchers claim that some 100 delegates and alternates in San Francisco were Birch Society members.) It grew during the campaign period when the Birchers, on the heels of Senator Goldwater's ringing defense of extremism, moved into the campaign and used it as a vehicle for their own special purposes of propaganda and recruitment. Birchers moved into the party in increasing numbers, and some party members moved into the Birch Society, in a cross-fertilization whose results have been apparent ever since: fattened Society strength and greater Birchite influence at the grass-roots levels of the GOP itself.

An example of this influence can be found in Birch pollution of the political atmosphere of southern California. In 1966:

• It was noted that three key officers of the California Young Republican organization were Birch Society members.

• An official of the conservative United Republicans of California stated that the group included in its membership 10% to 15% who were either Birch members or Birch sympathizers. Les Andrew, vice chairman of UROC in Southern California, denied that his organization had connections with "political extremism," though Andrew himself was an avowed member of the Birch Society.

• Five of the 16 top officials of the conservative California Republican Assembly were Birch Society members. The president of the CRA had previously defended Birchers against attacks by the national GOP leadership.

• John Rousselot, the Society's public relations director, held a seat on the Los Angeles County Central Republican Committee. (Rousselot had been an avowed Bircher when a member of the Congress of the United States.)

• Only a few days after a condemnation of the Birch Society by national Republican leaders in October, 1965, the Los Angeles County Young Republicans went on record in defense of the Society, shouting approval of a resolution which expressed "confidence that the John Birch Society is composed of loyal and concerned Americans."

The event that apparently led to a move, late in 1965, for a Republican Party repudiation of The John Birch Society was the entry of Bircher Richard Murphy into the Republican primary against incumbent Sen. Karl Mundt, of South Dakota, a staunch Republican conservative. Murphy announced in September, 1965, that he would challenge Mundt for the nomination in the 1966 primary. He conceded that Mundt was a conservative, but said the Senator had been far too liberal in his votes, favoring farm price support programs, civil rights, foreign aid, and federal aid to education.

(Mundt swamped Murphy when the primary votes were counted by four to one. During the campaign, Murphy quit the Society, claiming it was butting in and trying to control his bid for the nomination).

Less than a month later, Sen. Thruston Morton of Kentucky, former GOP National Chairman and himself a party moderate, declared in Washington:

As a partisan Republican, I am concerned by the fact that the John Birch Society has picked my party . . . as the vehicle to promulgate its monolithic philosophy.

There are three organizations in this country which give me grave doubts as a citizen: the Communist Party, the Ku Klux Klan, and the John Birch Society. Although their goals differ, they have one thing in common, and that is secrecy . . .

During the 1940's, the Communist Party tried to infiltrate the great Democratic Party. They didn't do it . . . What really concerns me is that a secret society should threaten and attempt to destroy one of our two great political parties. The Birchites label the late John Foster Dulles and Dr. Milton Eisenhower as Communists. They label General Dwight Eisenhower as a Communist sympathizer. They imply that Barry Goldwater is a Socialist. In my book, these men are great Americans. I don't think we have any room in the Republican Party for a clandestine organization engaged in character assassination.

Morton was also quoted as saying that "it's not the Birch membership I'm aiming at. Most of the members would be welcome into the Republican Party. But the leadership takes over the party at the precinct level. This is a threat to our party . . . you have to think their way—or you are out. They take over the precinct organization and if you are not with them, you are out."

A day later, Morton was joined in his denunciation by Sen. Everett Dirksen, the Senate minority leader, and by Rep. Gerald Ford, the House minority leader. A number of other Republican leaders issued statements—Gov. Mark Hatfield of Oregon, Sen. Jacob Javits of New York, Sen. Leverett Saltonstall of Massachusetts and others.

On November 5, 1965, at an Albuquerque news conference, Republican National Chairman Ray Bliss called on all Republicans to "reject membership in any radical organization which attempts to use the Republican Party for its own ends." Mr. Bliss did not identify the groups he referred

to, but he said "honest, patriotic and conscientious conservatives may be misjudged because of irresponsible radicals such as Robert Welch."

The reaction of the Birch leaders was predictable. Welch
charged that the outbreak of "Birch-baiting" had been
inspired by the Communists, who had now "initiated,
created and unleashed a campaign of attack against The
John Birch Society that makes all earlier attacks look like
mere pilot operations." (A *New York Times* report compared the Birch reaction to that of the Communists in the
1930s who cried "red-baiting" whenever their role in the
liberal movement of that day was exposed.)

The GOP Coordinating Committee met in Washington
on December 13, 1965, and adopted a resolution that,
while not naming the Birch Society specifically, endorsed
the strong position taken by Bliss at Albuquerque. It called
upon all Republicans to "reject membership in any radical
or extremist organization including any which attempts to
use the Republican Party for its own ends or any which
seeks to undermine the basic principles of American freedom and constitutional government."

Even in the face of such clear opposition from the top
GOP leaders, however, the Birch Society has continued in
its attempts to use the traditional party organizations for
its own ends—and in doing so, to involve its membership
in purely political action under the Birch banner.

The Activists

A flagrant example was the organized attempt on the
part of the entire extreme Right in California, during the
election campaign of 1966, to sweep from their state's
Supreme Court bench at least four of its seven justices.
Three of the judges had been condemned for having voted
to invalidate Proposition 14 (passed on the 1964 ballot),
which would have guaranteed the right of all property
owners to discriminate in the sale or rental of housing. The

146

offense of the fourth justice was that he had abstained in the crucial vote.

The openly political campaign against the four high judges was waged by the conservative California Republican Assembly and by a "Committee for a Responsible California Supreme Court"—and it was their undeniable right to do so. However, a political appeal from the second of these groups found its way into a memo sent to all Birch Society section leaders and chapter leaders in California by the Society's paid major coordinator, D. Richard Pine. The appeal for concerted *political* action was obvious, though the memo had been prefaced with this disclaimer:

> While this is *not a Society project*, it is being sent to you *for informational purposes* and for whatever action members wish to take *as individual citizens.*

The emphasis in the above has been added—pointing to the transparent phrases with which the Birch spokesmen attempted to mask a clear call for political action ("whatever action members wish to take . . ."). No section leader in Welch's organization, receiving the memo, would be likely to take its disclaimer seriously—that it was "not a Society project"—when its letterhead read:

THE JOHN BIRCH SOCIETY
West Coast Regional Office
2627 Mission Street,
San Marino, California, 91108.

The campaign to punish the justices failed by roughly two to one, but the effort was highly organized and those who sparked it showed plenty of political muscle in their unsuccessful endeavor, mobilizing more than a million votes for the removal of the four jurists who were their main targets.

Nor could it be regarded as merely the political action of "individual citizens" in Texas when the Republican

Committee of Harris County, which includes Houston, was threatened by total Birchite control, averted only by the personal intervention of such leading conservatives as Sen. John Tower and Peter O'Donnell, a leading Goldwater supporter in 1964.

There were other Birchite thrusts for power that could hardly be described as the work of "individual citizens." In the 1966 Michigan primary, a bloc of Birch-promoted candidates ran for precinct delegate posts in what one GOP leader called a "blatant grab for political power." Nor was the 1966 political in-fighting in Maricopa County, Arizona, purely the activity of "individuals." This was Barry Goldwater's home county, and the apparent victory of extremists in the local Republican organization prompted the 1964 Presidential candidate to declare, in an interview with the *Arizona Republic,* that "it was mostly Birchers there," and to warn of the serious consequences of any sizeable growth of Birchite influence in the State GOP.

Despite his credentials as a legitimate and a leading American conservative, Goldwater was not spared the wrath of certain Birchers after his criticism of Birchite political activities. In a recent letter, he said that when he was forced to "straighten out" that " 'family' fight," he was "immediately deluged with vitriolic letters." The strange thing, Goldwater said, was that "nearly all of them followed an exact pattern and many of them, coming from such faraway places as the New England States, Washington, and California, carried the precise language, word for word, that was later used to discredit me by my own County Chairman, a former Birch member." Goldwater concluded that "their letter writing and phone calls are closely directed and controlled from one single source."

The GOP has had its problems with Birchite infiltration elsewhere across the country—for example, in Wisconsin, Washington, Nevada, and North Dakota—and the Society has made inroads in several Southern states as well.

A resolution adopted by the Republican State Central Committee in Washington denounced the Society, declaring that the "Republican Party did not achieve greatness nor will it regain greatness by being the party of radicalism, or of the lunatic fringe." It added:

Such groups as the John Birch Society demonstrate by their methods, their leadership and their policies that they fail to meet the tests and follow the traditions of the Republican Party. They do not contribute to its victory but to its defeat; they do not strengthen it but weaken it; they do not effectively promote conservative principles, they subvert them.

The Birchite rule-or-ruin attitude toward the Republican Party was summed up by Birch Society National Council member Tom Anderson when he declared:

"I'm for making the Republican Party conservative or making it die."

The Society is, moreover, encouraging its members to run for political office—"on their own," of course.

The ideological atmosphere of California, especially Southern California, has produced the largest number of politically ambitious Birch Society activists. In the June, 1966, primaries, about a dozen known Birchers sought office and eight of them won Republican nominations. One of these ultimately did not make the race in November, and of the seven others, two were elected—both to the State Senate. One of the victors was H. L. Richardson, a former paid staff member of the Society, who said he had resigned his membership early in 1966 when he decided to seek election from the 19th Senatorial District. The other was State Sen. John G. Schmitz, a Bircher from Orange County, who had been elected in 1964 and was re-elected in 1966.

In Wisconsin, George Klicka, an avowed Society member, was elected to the State Assembly from suburban Wauwatosa and Kenneth J. Merkel won re-election after serving one two-year term. Klicka's win over his Democratic opponent was an impressive three to one.

149

A similar lopsided victory was scored in Utah by Bircher J. Reese Hunter, who was elected to the lower house of the legislature by almost four to one. And in Alaska, C. R. Lewis, identified as a Birch member by Founder Welch himself, was elected to the State Senate, although Dr. Lee McKinley, also a Bircher, was defeated in his bid for the U. S. Senate by incumbent Democrat E. L. Bartlett.

In Florida, Bernard Klassen was elected as a member of the lower house of the State Legislature, and a month after his victory, was introduced by Founder Welch at the Birch Society's Eighth Annual Birthday Dinner in New York.

At the local level, Birchers here and there were successful in bids for public office. In Montebello, Calif., for instance, Dr. Bruce Odou, a Society section leader, was elected as Mayor—Birch Public Relations Director Rousselot, declaring that Birchers are being urged to play a more active role in politics than ever before, said Odou's election showed what could be accomplished. And in Middleboro, Mass., Leo F. Kahian, a leading Bircher who once described the United Nations as a "diabolical, satanic, Godless monstrosity," was elected as a town selectman after flaunting his Birch membership before the voters.

In a discussion of the 1966 elections which appeared in the December issue of the members' *Bulletin*, Welch recalled some of his statements at the founding meeting of the Society, which were quoted from the *Blue Book* at the beginning of this chapter.

Welch said that in the eight years since the Society was founded, "we have learned a great deal"—most important that "we do not need nor want a million members within the United States." Welch declared that between 300,000 and 400,000 members, "with the same dedication as those we now have," would give the Society "adequate influence to change the frightening present course of our Ship of State." Welch said that more than 400,000 members "would give us power instead of influence" and he added that "power is entirely too dangerous a weapon in the possession of any voluntary association."

After that disclaimer, Welch boasted that the Society had "proved what can be done by our educational program, and in the elections of 1966 this potential . . . was made entirely obvious to any part of the general public which is willing to study the results."

Insisting, as he had over the years, that the Society itself "is *not* a political organization," Welch went on to tell of the impact made by his group on the voting patterns in various parts of the country. "The elections just past," he wrote, "did a great deal to prove our point, and to show how much our strategy had accomplished even with the comparatively small numerical size we have yet been able to reach."

Welch claimed that "the election returns would have been far different in California, and Idaho, and Utah, and Alaska, and North Dakota, and Florida, and many other places, but for the understanding of issues, and awareness of the dangers facing our country, which members of The John Birch Society have played so large a part in bringing about."

In Idaho, Welch wrote, the Society was "fairly strong" and its members "had been actively carrying on our educational program for several years." Two leading anti-Birch Republicans, Gov. Robert Smylie and former Rep. Ralph Harding, were on the ballot, Smylie seeking re-election, Harding seeking a seat in the U.S. Senate. Yet, Welch crowed, both lost—"and there was practically a clean sweep throughout the state for the whole conservative cause."

In California, Welch said, the Birch Society itself "took absolutely no part or position in the campaign" but a "preponderant majority of our members undoubtedly worked for Reagan, and Brown gradually made Birch support of Reagan the chief issue in the whole campaign for the governorship."

151

But, Welch declared, "the really important point to be remembered" was "the underlying development which made it possible for Ronald Reagan (however 'moderate' at heart he may be or may become) to run, be nominated, and be elected *as a Conservative.*"

Welch told his members (and the world) that the "sharp change in the California political climate during the last very few years, was due in large part to the untiring educational work of thousands of members of The John Birch Society." He added:

> We had chosen California as a state in which to concentrate practically from the beginning. As a rule, about fifteen percent of the total field staff we could afford, and hence at least fifteen percent of our total membership, has been in California. So, while the labor and contributions of individual Birchers on behalf of Reagan undoubtedly helped, it was the Birch educational program, carried on steadily for years, especially in southern California, which had helped so mightily to make a Reagan campaign even possible in the first place.

Welch also claimed that Birch Society activity was a major factor in the defeat of the civilian-controlled police review board in New York City.

> Our members did their work so well, especially in bringing other patriotic Americans into ad hoc committees to help them, and the *Support Your Local Police* theme was gradually understood, accepted, and backed by so much of the public, that most supporters of the drive today do not even know that it was started and given substance by an educational project of The John Birch Society.

The way such efforts can produce results at the polls, Welch said, "was never shown more clearly than by the vote" on the civilian review board question in New York on November 8, 1966.

The same thing, the Founder told his followers, "will

152

be true with regard to other subjects, and in other areas, to whatever extent we can create sufficient understanding."

Welch said "detailed analysis of many other election returns" would also demonstrate the impact which had been made by the Society on the 1966 political scene. Moreover, he said that what the Birchers had set out to do *"can be done"*—and he told the faithful, as he had in *Looking Ahead,* early in 1965, that "all it would take . . . is enough Coordinators, and hence eventually enough members and enough activities, in about 325 Congressional Districts, to do the job and achieve the same results we have already accomplished spottily in some areas. And," Welch wrote, "we are hoping that the 'proofs of the pudding,' as given by the 1966 elections, will now enable us to move ahead rapidly in that direction."

What the Society needed was "more patriots"—and the founder said "we need them soon."

The John Birch Society, in short, was conceived by Welch eight years ago as a political organization. It is political in its goal of reversing "the whole new-deal march toward state socialism" and expunging the "disease of collectivism," as Welch defined it at Indianapolis in 1958.

And, as Welch has on a number of occasions reminded his members, the Birch Society, as a new kind of political organization, does not, "like a political party, fall to pieces as soon as an election is over, and have to be painfully reassembled and then enthused before the next one. We are not, as are so many political organizations, so loosely and tenuously held together that we resemble a gaseous fog far more than a solid body." And, Welch went on, the Society doesn't have "goals and purposes that are constantly swaying and shifting with changing political winds, and which are being repeatedly modified and compromised to fit the transient shades of political expediency of various candidates."

Welch is, moreover, on solid ground in claiming, as he has, that the Birchers "wield an influence on any political scene far out of proportion to their numbers." The Society nevertheless continues to hide its political activity under an "educational" camouflage. Yet its goal remains what it has been all along—to put its weight into the political scales in the United States "just as fast and far" as it can. To do so, as Founder Welch said eight years ago, it seeks to "use politicians, support politicians, create, politicians" —and yet for eight years Welch has been denying that he founded and still heads a political organization—an organization which, like the Communist Party, seeks to create a political climate in which victories for candidates of its liking will follow as a plain matter of course.

CHAPTER TWELVE

Program and Activities

The peculiar John Birch view of reality—the United States seen as 60%-80% Communist-controlled, of nineteenth century America as some sort of idyllic pinnacle of civilization, and most subsequent American history as the disastrous result of diabolical conspiracies—has attracted significant numbers of Right Wing radicals. It has produced, necessarily, a program to satisfy needs that have obviously led to successful organization. Officially, action is limited to the dissemination of a barrage of propaganda—books, flyers, tapes, records, films, rally speeches, petitions, and bumper stickers—to the infiltration of various civic, political, church, and school organizations, to the formation of front committees and to the writing of letters. But often action has taken more subtle and disturbing forms under the traditional Birch mantle of secrecy and the Welch dictum that justifies the use at times of "mean and dirty" tactics.

The National Activities

Some analysts have suggested that the Society's national program amounts to little more than the hard recruiting of new members—that all else is propaganda developed for recruitment purposes. In any event, the Society's basic biases have spawned certain causes and crusades which form the

155

framework of its national effort. To this framework are hung the local front groups, the flood of pseudo-educational materials disseminated through a network of bookstores, and the loyalties of the members themselves.

The Society's early scattered shots at enemies far and wide have been gradually narrowed down to selected targets described in the Standard Agenda in the massive November, 1965, *Bulletin*. It is into this agenda, with only slight variations, that the national program has been jelled:

    I. Recruiting . . .
    II. The Movement to Impeach Warren . . .
    III. The United Nations—Get US Out . . .
    IV. Civil Rights . . .
    V. The Liberty Amendment . . .
       (abolish income tax)
    VI. Support Your Local Police . . .
    VII. American Opinion . . .
    VIII. American Opinion Libraries . . .
    IX. American Opinion Speakers Bureau . . .
    X. Conduct Study Clubs . . .
    XI. The Review of the News . . .
    XII. Your Own Reading . . .

The *Bulletin* urges support for some of the above items (e.g., Liberty Amendment) and damnation for others (e.g., Civil Rights). In addition, a series of temporary projects often follows—a torrent of letters to some unsuspecting senator, perhaps, or greeting cards to a Welch hero.

The Attack on the UN

The John Birch Society has been the principal Radical Rightist organization in the United States attacking the United Nations. Under Welch's leadership, the Society has mounted an extensive and ongoing campaign against the United Nations and its specialized agencies. The chief JBS propaganda slogan has been "Get the US out of the

UN and the UN out of the US." Of recent date, this has been simplified to "Get US out!"—the slogan that, as stated previously, sometimes has been taken to refer to Vietnam.

Since the September, 1963, issue of the Society's monthly *Bulletin* to members, the third Standard Agenda item has regularly been "The United Nations—Get US Out!" This call to action has been preceded in importance only by the constantly repeated Society request for "Recruiting" new and fallen-away members and for support of the "Movement to Impeach [Earl] Warren," the Chief Justice of the United States.

Thus, informing the American people of the purported "truth" about the United Nations has long been one of the major propaganda undertakings of The John Birch Society. But the "plain unvarnished truth," as Robert Welch sees it and repeats it over and over again, is that "The UN was *conceived* by Communists. The UN was *created* by Communists. The UN is *controlled* by Communists [and] The UN has constantly furthered the objectives of Communism."

Robert Welch wrote in the JBS *Bulletin* for May, 1965, that "there are more Communists in the United Nations building in New York than there are in the Kremlin." In the November, 1965, *Bulletin,* he said that "most of the Communist control of the United Nations is through Moscow's new African and Asian puppets." Welch added sarcastically that these countries "might average perhaps twenty bathtubs per nation," but that each one has a vote in the UN equal to that of the United States.

In harmony with the views of the Society's founder, Rousselot, the Birch Public Relations Director, once stated that "The UN was originally designed and planned by key Communist sympathizers, and today the organization is controlled and administered by the Communists." When Rousselot made this charge in a speech at the July, 1965, Birch-dominated Rally for God and Country in Boston,

Mass., G. Edward Griffin, a Society official from California, who is director of the Society's audio-visual department, commented: "He's read my book."

Griffin's book, *The Fearful Master,* has been one of the Birch Society's chief weapons in its propaganda assault on the United Nations.

The author, comparing Americans to suicidal lemmings, writes that in supporting the United Nations, the United States "abandoned the secure ground of national strength and independence to leap into the boiling waters of internationalism." He sees the UN itself as a nest of spies and Communist murderers, says that loyalty to the UN is being designed to supplant loyalty to the United States, and that the loyalty eventually demanded will be to world Communism. These facts, he concludes, are all hidden from the American people because the UN, like all enemies of the Birch Society, is secret and conspiratorial.

Acknowledging that the greatest effectiveness of The John Birch Society in influencing public opinion has usually been achieved through the workings of "ad hoc" committees—front groups—Welch recently urged the immediate formation of local or regional committees "To Restore American Independence Now" (TRAIN). The JBS leader initially proposed the idea of establishing these anti-UN committees in the Society's *Bulletin* for May, 1966.

TRAIN committees soon thereafter sprang up in a number of communities across the country. If the TRAIN committees prove to be as widespread and as active as the Society's TACT committees, they will undoubtedly be an element to be watched in the months and years to come.

The latest anti-UN propaganda produced by The John Birch Society is a 29-minute film strip on the world organization, directed by John Rousselot and narrated by G. Edward Griffin. Welch has recommended it for use by the Society's TRAIN committees and for showing to service clubs and similar audiences. The film-strip narration is also available separately on either tape recording or a long-playing record.

Other anti-UN materials of the Society include postcards, which label the UN building "The House That Hiss Built"; stickers of various sizes bearing the slogan "Get US Out!", which are available for envelopes or auto bumpers; and a special $2 packet of propaganda materials which includes, among other things, the Griffin book and a purported exposé of the World Health Organization (WHO) by the late J. B. Matthews.

Another recently compiled "Packet for Politicians and other Patriotic and Public Spirited Citizens" offers two books on the subject of the United Nations—Griffin's *The Fearful Master* and *46 Angry Men,* a report prepared by civilian doctors of Elizabethville containing "a documented, illustrated survey of the atrocities committed by United Nations troops during the 1961 attack on Katanga."

Welch stated in his introduction to the *American Opinion* reprint of *46 Angry Men*:

> There are still millions of honorable people, even otherwise well informed people, throughout the world who believe—as these forty-six doctors believed a year ago— that there is some good in the United Nations. We ourselves believe that it is simply an instrumentality in the International Communist Conspiracy's plan of global conquest.
>
> We believe that today the United Nations organization is almost completely controlled by the Communists; and that those who infest the upended ant box on the East River are just as cruel, murderous, ruthless, and rotten as are their counterparts in other instrumentalities of Soviet power and propaganda, wherever found.

Letter-Writing Campaigns

The Birch Society's national anti-UN campaign has included several massive letter-writing efforts. In the November, 1964, *Bulletin,* Welch requested that JBS members bombard Mrs. Norman Chandler, Walt Disney, and other directors of the newly established Los Angeles Music Center with mail protesting a decision to fly the UN flag over the project. For whatever reason, the flag did not fly, and Welch crowed of a victory.

Also in 1964, and continuing into 1965, as a result of the Xerox Corporation's announced sponsorship of a projected series of television specials dramatizing the work of various UN agencies, the Birch Society declared war on the internationally known copying-machine company. Founder Welch urged JBS members to send "a veritable flood" of letters to the company protesting their decision.

Even before the first program reached the television screen, Xerox had already received 29,500 pieces of adverse mail. A tabulation made by the company revealed, however, that the 29,500 letters had been sent by only 6,000 individuals. In the six-month period that followed, during which time Welch wrote several reminders to his membership, the company received another 15,700 adverse letters, which were analyzed as having come from only 5,500 individuals. During the same period, Xerox received a total of 11,600 favorable letters from about 11,600 individuals.

The end result of the affair was that the Xerox Corporation went ahead with its sponsorship of the programs and refused to be intimidated by the Birchers. This, as the Gloucester, Mass., *Times* editorially noted, despite the fact that "such an avalanche of letters would have scared many small businesses right out of their profit-minded wits."

The Movement to Impeach Earl Warren

The "Movement to Impeach Earl Warren" in 1966 continued to be a major Birch Society project even though Welch advised his members, in the May, 1966, *Bulletin,* to "put the project temporarily on a back burner . . ."

He said he wanted to "keep it simmering" while the Society used "the front burner full force to bring other projects to a boil."

Nevertheless, in January, 1967, Welch told his followers to "keep the gas turned on" and that the Society expected "to start this pot really boiling again in only two or three more months." At a press conference in Los Angeles on January 11th, Welch explained that the Society had, until then, been engaged in a relatively low-keyed, academic campaign on the Warren impeachment issue. The contemplated new program, he told newsmen, would be an intensive, organized national drive to work through the House of Representatives for impeachment of the Chief Justice.

Low-key, high-key, back burner or front, the Birchite project to oust the nation's highest ranking justice has been a part of the Society's program ever since it was founded in 1958.

There are hundreds of large "Impeach Earl Warren" billboards on streets, roads, and highways all across the country, paid for by zealous local Birchers. Visitors to the Indianapolis Speedway on Memorial Day, 1965, for instance, could not miss the huge sign opposite the entrance. It advised:

SAVE OUR REPUBLIC. IMPEACH EARL WARREN!

The mammoth advertising space had been contracted for by a local group calling itself the "Committee for Outdoor Advertising to Save Our Republic."

A similar sign greeted civil rights marchers just outside the city of Selma, Ala., during their famous march early in 1965. There, the billboard was signed "The John Birch Society."

The Birchers' appeal in the Selma area was, intentionally or not, to certain obvious emotions. Indeed, later, in the November, 1965, *Bulletin,* Welch stated:

. . . the Chief Justice seems to us to be more responsible than any other man for making possible the lawlessness now being brazenly paraded as "civil rights." So that even in concentration spreading the truth about "civil rights," in many instances our members will automatically be spreading the information and reasons why Warren should be impeached.

But the official purposes of the Birchites' now-famous "Movement to Impeach Earl Warren" are much broader. Welch stated in the November, 1965, *Bulletin*:

Let's not forget that Warren will simply have to be impeached, as a warning to other judges of the lower courts as well as of the Supreme Court, before we can ever return this country to a rule of law instead of the rule of men. It is now at the mercy of those who happen to be in control of the law enforcement machinery at any particular place or time.

Earlier, Welch wrote in the March, 1965, *Bulletin* that the proposal to impeach the Chief Justice of the United States was intended "to make men behave, not to give them more laws to distort and ignore. And the way to make the Justices on the present Supreme Court behave is to impeach the ringleader in their judicial crimes . . ."

In May, 1965, Welch assessed the effort: "If and when we can make enough good citizens informed enough and aroused enough to force the impeachment of Warren, we shall have won a battle of tremendous importance in the total war." In short, the Society wants to persuade "good citizens" that the court of ultimate appeal in this country today is besmirched by terrible treason. The idea was expressed in an unsigned article in the July-August, 1965, issue of *American Opinion:*

The theory that the Warren Court is working for a domestic, as distinct from foreign, dictatorship becomes less tenable every day.

To advance the idea of such infamy in high places the

162

Birch Society sells a Warren Impeachment Packet—a $2.45 bundle of propaganda for $1, which includes the Robert Welch leaflet, *Republics and Democracies* (condemning democracy), and two pamphlets by Mississippi's Senator James O. Eastland (one entitled *Is the Supreme Court Pro-Communist?*).

Welch continually urges circulation of the packet, of a series of *Dan Smoot Reports* on the same subject, and of a one-page compendium entitled *Why Warren Should Be Impeached*—all explanations of "the role played by Earl Warren in the destruction of our republic." The large billboard posters displayed at Selma and elsewhere across the land are available through Society headquarters at $20.

In addition, in the October, 1966, *Bulletin,* Welch indicated that the Society was "waiting for a forthcoming book, which will supply basic support for an all-out drive on this project." He urged in the meantime that members continue their anti-Warren effort, thereby "preparing the way—and the day."

Repeal the Income Tax

The opposition of the Birch Society to the Federal Income Tax is rooted in the belief of Founder Welch that the Sixteenth Amendment to the U.S. Constitution is part of the long-range, insidious plot to convert the United States into a Marxist-style collective society.

Thus it is that Welch urges his members to cooperate in every way with the Liberty Amendment Committee, headed by Willis E. Stone, whose main activity is an ongoing effort to get state legislatures to adopt resolutions urging repeal of the Income Tax Amendment.

During 1966, however, the Birch Society added to its own complex of arms and apparatuses another group dedicated to the repeal of the income tax. The group was the Organization for Repeal of the Federal Income Tax Inc. (ORFIT) which was formed in 1953 and which had merged with Stone's organization in the late 1950s. The merger was short-lived, however, and little was heard of ORFIT in the years that followed. It was headed, at least for a time, by D. B. Lewis, the pet food manufacturer who died in 1966 and whose will bequeathed Dan Smoot and the Birch Society $1,000,000 each.

At any rate, in March, 1966, Welch announced to his members that "we have now brought ORFIT into the family as one of our affiliated organizations." He added that "we intend to publish some books and pamphlets under the name of this Organization for Repeal of the Federal Income Tax" and in the meantime, he urged the faithful to continue cooperation with Stone's group.

The Community Level

The influence of The John Birch Society—and of the Radical Right in general—is often most effective, most easily seen, and most keenly felt at the grass-roots level of American life. It is in the community that their political plans and their hopes to reverse the direction of American life and government—and even of world affairs—must inevitably begin. It is at the local level—in hundreds of cities, suburbs, towns and hamlets—that the 4,000 Birch chapters and the 80,000 or so Birch members have been feverishly toiling in recent years.

Robert Welch believes in the importance of local community groups, civic organizations and voluntary committees in American life. He seems to feel that the Birchers must penetrate and influence these vital sinews of American life if the Society is to achieve the counter-thrust it seeks at the national level—to repeal American political, social, and economic history since 1933—or even since 1913.

The Birch need for effective strength at the local level is obvious:

• Infiltration and the capture of positions of influence are more easily accomplished, and ultimately more effective, at the local level. The position of public librarian in the town of Boxford, Mass., for example, was held by a Birch member who had done public recruiting and organizing work for the Society. She lost her job after using it to promote the distribution of Birch literature through the library.

• The apathy of moderates is more in evidence, and offers more potent an opportunity for an extremist minority, at the local level. Turnouts for community or school board elections, for example, are notoriously low almost everywhere.

• There is a greater emotional pull on issues that "hit home"—particularly when the emotions can be buttressed with a manufactured fear, or where neighborhoods are split in bitterness.

• Greater political pressure, concentrated and personal, can be brought to bear on local, county and state officials, and on local businessmen.

• Pressures can be tightly organized, and it is easy to mount saturation propaganda drives reaching great percentages of the local population.

For example, in the Washington, D.C.-Maryland area, where substantial Birch Society growth has taken place, activity is energetic and well-financed. A heavy volume of Birchite propaganda is distributed through local book outlets. The membership has influential friends at state and county legislative levels. In the Baltimore area, Birchers and their allies were instrumental in campaigns to kill an urban renewal program and various poverty program projects. In several Maryland counties they have been able to distribute Society materials to teachers in the schools. This is typical of Birch effectiveness on the local community level.

"Front" Groups

A major Birch activity in communities from coast to coast has been the establishment of front groups—often used as cloaks of respectability or anonymity—through which the national programs of the Society can be adapted to the local scene and new members lured into cooperation first and recruitment later. Very often these are committees named as being in "support of the police," or of "law and order," or of "God in our schools." Many have been called the "Committee to Get the US out of the UN"—although under the Birch drive for respectability, a New England group of that name became the "Committee to Promote Understanding of the United Nations." There are, likewise, many committees "to Impeach Earl Warren"—but one in California's San Gabriel Valley has become the "Committee for Judicial Re-Education."

The "Southeastern Massachusetts Educational Committee" originally had but one educational activity—it showed a Birch Society recruiting film in and around the city of Taunton. It now also sponsors the Society's radio show, heard weekly on a local station.

In newspaper advertisements, the Wakefield (Mass.) Forum not long ago announced a lecture series under its sponsorship at the Wakefield Memorial High School. The Forum did not identify itself as a Birch operation. But a local citizen, whose only Far Right link had been his registration on July 4, 1965, at Boston's Rally for God and Country (which itself had officially denied Birch Society affiliation), received a mailing from the Society's national headquarters in September. It included a handful of Birch literature, an application for tickets to the Wakefield Forum, and a map showing routes to the Wakefield High School.

The American Opinion Forum of Long Island (N. Y.), which also sponsored a series of "conservative" speakers, was more obvious. Its usherettes wore uniforms emblazoned with a gold-embroidered "JBS."

The purpose of such committees and forums is to expose the public to Birch ideology with the aim of recruitment—usually under the cloak of some righteous-sounding cause.

166

The chairman of Connecticut's "Christian Committee for Prayers in Schools," for example, was The John Birch Society's paid state coordinator.

By infiltrating community organizations—school, civic, and church groups—and by harassing those it cannot dominate, or those of an opposing viewpoint (such as those fostering civil rights, civil liberties, or the UN), the local Birch apparatus seeks to gain that measure of grass-roots control that is the necessary base of power.

Attempted Takeovers

When a number of residents in Mount Prospect, Ill., called a preliminary meeting for the formation of a human relations council, the local Birch chapter leader (Chapter QRKJ) alerted all Society members in the area to the potential danger of "left-wingers." The Birchers showed up in strength at an organizational meeting of the new anti-bias group, packing its membership. They managed to have their own people elected to office—some of whom had opposed formation of the council in the first place—and appointed to draft the proposed by-laws. They made it clear they wanted the organization to take a strong stand against race-mixing ("mongrelizing"), to watch out for Communists, and perhaps to dissolve itself. Thus, a genuine community effort to improve relations between the races, and between persons of different religions, was to be made a shambles by the infiltration and tactics of John Birch Society members.

Late in November, 1965, a public meeting was called in Saratoga, Calif., to discuss ways to establish an advisory board of directors for an area center of the poverty program. Establishment of the board was a necessary step toward setting up the area center, and the meeting had been called by an ad hoc committee for the district, which included more than a half-dozen communities. Close to 250 persons were present, including several prominent members of The John Birch Society in the area, and when the voting came, it appeared that at least two-thirds of the audience were Birchers or their fellow-travelers. The Birchers elected all 18 members of the Advisory Board.

The Birchers and their allies attempted takeovers, both in Mount Prospect and at Saratoga. In other communities across the nation, they have attacked on wider fronts. A case in point: Nashua, N.H. There the local Birchers operate through a front organization called the Southern New Hampshire Forum for American Opinion, Inc., which has helped fan the ideological fires by bringing to town a parade of speakers from the Birch bureau including Tom Anderson of the Birch Society Council, Julia Brown, Willis Stone, and Harold Lord Varney. They have been aided in their activities by the presence of a Nashua outlet of the Let Freedom Ring telephone message service.

Another local outlet for the Birch line has been the letters-to-the-editor columns of the Manchester *Union-Leader,* which have seen long essays in thousands of words contributed by local Society members and coordinators. Even the Rightist-oriented editorial column of *Union-Leader* publisher William Loeb, however, penetrated what it called the "sham" of the Southern New Hampshire Forum's name, declaring: "This is The John Birch Society. That's a fact, not our opinion."

For a time, after the 1964 election, the Young Republican Club in Nashua had come under the domination of Birchers, who brought Samuel Blumenfeld to address the club. Blumenfeld, then an editor of the Birchite Western Islands book publishing operation and now Analysis Editor of the Birch weekly, *Review of the News,* ripped apart the Warren Commission that investigated the assassination of President Kennedy, and the YR Club had to pay $165 and expenses to hear him do it. The appearance of Blumenfeld, who believes that democracy is all wrong and promises it will be replaced "when and if The John Birch Society becomes a dominant political force in America," was a factor in a subsequent revolt by anti-Birch YRs, many of them members of the local Junior Chamber of Commerce, who formed the Greater Nashua Better Government Council and ousted the Birchers and their allies from control of the club in 1965.

Some Birch-minded individuals favor action. A Catholic priest in North Attleboro, Mass., who advised his parishioners not to attend a lecture by Father Francis Fenton, a member of the Birch National Council, became the target of abusive telephone calls and a whispering campaign. In Santa Barbara, Calif., a reporter who had exposed local Birch Society activities had his automobile tires slashed by an unknown culprit.

"AC Study Clubs"

The launching of a new Birchite operation called the AC Study Clubs, designed as permanent groups meeting weekly under Birch leadership, was announced by Welch in the October, 1966, *Bulletin*. "AC", Welch explained, can stand for "American Conservative" Study Club, "American Constitution" Study Club, "Anti-Communist" Study Club, or any other names to which the initials "AC" lend themselves.

Welch suggested that two or three Birchers act together to form an AC Study Club, and then bring in ten or twelve non-Birchers to complete the unit. The aim, he said, was to get citizens "who are now intuitively grasping the truth [to] become active participants in our *Operation Exposure,* without waiting until they are ready to join the Society." Welch noted that "a considerable help to recruiting of excellent new [Birch Society] members will undoubtedly result from the growth and spread of AC Study Clubs."

Welch has instructed his members to answer anyone asking if the new front is a Birch operation: "You bet it is!"

Schools and PTAs

Birch members and other extremists use the democratic processes to harass local school boards and municipal governments.

A campaign begun by religious organizations in New Jersey to persuade schools and other municipal buildings to fly a pennant reading "One Nation Under God," together with the American Flag, aroused bitter controversies in some communities. It was seen by some as an effort to circumvent—or even to thumb the community nose at—rulings of the Supreme Court on questions of the separation of church and state. The Bergen, N.J., *Record* disclosed that the sale of the "religious" pennants was a major local operation of Birch Society units, netting a new American Opinion bookstore in Bergen County some $200 weekly.

School boards and parent-teacher associations have been a prime target of other Radical Rightist pressures on the community level in the last two or three years. The National Education Association has estimated that one school district in every 30 "experienced some sort of attack, opposition or attempt to infiltrate the schools by the extremists and dissident critics."

A report presented by a commission of the N.E.A. at a January, 1966, conference on "Critics and the Schools" summarized responses to a questionnaire sent to nearly 15,000 teachers and other educators. The Birch Society was cited as the school's Number One troublemaker. (The Society also was number 20 on a list of groups said to be helpful to the schools.)

In Carmichael, Calif., a local Birch Society member presented a petition to the school board demanding that a certain American history textbook be withdrawn as "subversive." She cited *American Opinion* poet E. Merrill Root as her expert authority. The Carmichael *Courier* reported that after her speech before the board, the lady—representing a "Committee for the Return of Morality"—screamed at the president of the local teachers' association that she would see him "burn in hell" because of his opposition to extremist views.

In the August, 1966, *Bulletin* Welch promoted a non-Birch California corporation called Youth of America Needs to Know (YANK), whose program consists of placing a standardized collection of 50 hardbound books, chosen from the Birch Society's recommended list, in every high school in the United States. "Far from meeting any resistance to these gifts from school authorities," Welch noted, "they have found almost every high school quite avid to receive a YANK Library free." Welch urged members of the Society to support YANK to the best of their ability, although it was not part of the Birch organization itself.

In East Whittier, Calif., in May, 1966, the local school board was obliged to discharge a teacher, who was a member of the Birch Society, for "non-objective" teaching and for instilling "fear and prejudice in presenting controversial matters" to her sixth grade class. The teacher had been charged, among other things, with telling her students and the school principal that Negroes were "inferior" and with calling Dr. Martin Luther King a "Communist" and Vice-President Hubert H. Humphrey a "socialist."

Also in California, the President of the State Board of Education in early 1966 charged that the influence of the Birch Society had reached "poisonous proportions" in the Monrovia School District. He listed the Monrovia district as one of ten school districts throughout the state where the Society was allegedly "overtly or covertly at work." The allegations were denied by local school officials.

In October, 1966, the Society was criticized by the President of St. Vincent College in Latrobe, Pa., for allegedly curtailing a forum at which a Communist Party member was to have spoken. The school reduced its scheduled four-day symposium to one day after a bomb scare and a mass demonstration. The Rev. Maynard J. Brennan, President of the College, which is run by the Benedictine Order,

171

said that radio announcements sponsored by the Birch Society had called for the demonstration "to keep these Reds away from our campuses."

Join the PTA

In 1960, Welch advised his followers to "join your local PTA at the beginning of the school year, get your conservative friends to do likewise, and go to work to take it over." Birchers around the country have been doing so, and the Society has reaped a whirlwind of adverse publicity and public hostility from mothers across the land who devote countless hours to sincere PTA work.

When the adverse publicity mounted, Rousselot—in February, 1965—wrote to the Christian Science *Monitor,* which had published an Associated Press dispatch under the headline "PTA Tells of Extremist Pressures." Blandly ignoring Welch's September, 1960, plea that Birchers should take over local PTAs, Rousselot admitted that members were encouraged to join PTAs, but "not because the society has any intention of taking over . . ."

Rousselot said that the Birchers wanted only to expose the PTA "to conservative thinking." He argued that "liberal elements within the PTA should welcome the ideological competition which results from contact with conservatives." Adding that the Society had "never encouraged society members to foment discord within the PTA," he said, members were counselled at all times to be "morally correct and in every way decent."

Exactly how local Birchers carried out these strictures was, perhaps, exemplified in Upper Saddle River, N.J., where Birchers, in the face of public indifference, seized control of the local PTA. While there was some indication that clashing personalities may have been involved, it was also a fact that the man who had been nominated for PTA president had been active in interracial activities. As the PTA election approached, he was made the subject of a whispering campaign—that he was a "nigger-lover." At the election meeting, a large proportion of Birchers and their allies were present; most PTA members were not. The Presidency and the Vice-Presidency went to Birch Society members. Happily, the publicity alerted indifferent PTA members who, in the year the Birchers held office, effectively restrained them.

This episode suggests that the Birchers can be successful not only in capturing other PTAs, but even in taking them out of the PTA national organization, as has, in fact, happened.

The Birch view of the PTA was, perhaps, spelled out in recorded telephone messages broadcast by the Let Freedom Ring stations. LFR said that the PTA was Communist-infiltrated.

National PTA President Mrs. Jennelle Moorhead has reported that tactics of intimidation, coercion, and misrepresentation by Birchers and other extremists have become commonplace. She said that in her opinion, "these extremists are not really after the PTA but are attempting to gain control of it to get at their real objective—the educational system." The National PTAs have sent materials to local units to help them combat extremism—both Far Left and Birch-type Right.

The Attacks on UNICEF

UNICEF—the UN Children's Fund—is also a target of the Birchers, who have zeroed in on the Halloween "trick or treat" collections which schoolchildren make to bring in coins for UNICEF.

In Needham, Mass., on Halloween, 1965, a local Bircher gave some children boxes of candy with a telephone number on a sticker affixed to the boxes. The number was for the local Let Freedom Ring, the Radical Right telephone message propaganda operation. Those who called the number heard an attack on UNICEF and a plug for the Birch

173

book on the UN by G. Edward Griffin. The Needham *Chronicle* commented in a subsequent editorial that "far from what the talker would have the listener believe, UNICEF is not a communist-dominated organization, but an international humanitarian group . . . recipient of the Nobel Peace Prize." (In 1965, UNICEF received the Nobel Peace Prize for having helped hundreds of millions of children in more than 100 countries throughout the world.)

The same evening in Long Beach, Calif., extremists hung effigies—one with a "Murdered by UNICEF" sign pinned to its chest—in front of a pro-UN group's chapter office, a local radio station, and in the lobby of the building housing the community newspaper. A black coffin and anti-UN material were also circulated. The coffin contained bumper strips which read "Give Red China our U.N. seat." "Get U.S. out of U.N." "Help Get U.S. out of U.N."

The Long Beach *Press-Telegram* reported that letterheads and return addresses found on some of the material indicated that they had apparently emanated from the local Birchite American Opinion Library, and also from the Rightist Long Beach Freedom Forum.

More recently, in late October, 1966, the Dallas, Texas, *Times Herald* disclosed that local members of the Birch Society sponsored and financed a telephone recorded service which attacked UNICEF and again advised listeners to send for Griffin's anti-UN book. The newspaper reported that the address provided was that of the Dallas regional office of the Birch Society and its adjoining American Opinion Library.

Birchers have also protested the display and sale of UNICEF Christmas cards. In December, 1964, officials of two banks and a department store in Pacific Grove, Calif., reported that threats of picketing of their establishments by JBS members forced them to discontinue sale of UNICEF Christmas cards. A local Birch Society leader denied that picketing had been threatened. He acknowledged, however, that he had complained about the sale of the cards, whose receipts, he asserted, go in part to Communist countries.

At Falmouth, Mass., on Cape Cod, a local Birch leader persuaded the Pilgrim Youth Fellowship of the First Congregational Church, consisting of high school students, to vote against supporting the 1965 UNICEF drive in the community.

A somewhat broader effort by the Birchers to reach American youth took place on a national scale in the fall of 1965. Each of the Society chapters was asked to distribute —to college freshmen—25 copies of *None Dare Call It Treason,* the paperback book by John Stormer, charging the national administrations of the last 30 years with treason. In line with Welch's suggestion, Society members sent a personal note to each freshman recipient, urging that he read the Stormer book "to get some idea . . . of the true state of affairs in the world and his own country as against optimistic and deceptive twaddle he is so likely to be fed in most of the academic halls of today."

Attacks on the Press

Another American institution that has been the target of Birchers and other Radical Rightists is the nation's free press. In November, 1964, the California Newspaper Publishers Association found it necessary to launch a long-range campaign against "right-wing and left-wing attempts to discredit newspapers and other news media."

A report by a CNPA committee that studied the problem said in part:

Members of the John Birch Society and other extreme right-wing groups have joined the long list of left-wing extremist groups which have, for at least a generation, vigorously and viciously attacked the integrity of the reporting in the press, have attempted to discredit and damage economically newspapers with which they disagree and have sought to bring into being more news media which will be subservient in reflecting their own prejudices.

The report said the attacks were particularly acute during the 1964 Presidential campaign, but added that there was "abundant evidence that the derogation [of newspapers] will not end after the election . . ."

Two months earlier, publishers H. H. Ridder of the Long Beach *Independent* and L. Finder of the Sacramento *Union* told the Publishers Association of anti-press efforts by both extremes, but characterized the campaign of the ultra-Right John Birch Society and Birch-connected affiliates as most effective and most dangerous. Jack Baldwin of the Long Beach *Independent* confirmed their findings in his report on a nationwide investigation he and a colleague had conducted over a period of eight months.

Ridder, Finder and Baldwin said the attack on the press was in two parts. First, *Editor & Publisher* reported, "is a general attack on all of the press that is not under the control of the John Birch Society. Second is the picking off of one paper at a time and attempted intimidation to force submission to the organization's dictation."

The three newsmen cited wide-ranging tactics used by extremists against the press. These included: "vituperative letters, threatening boycotts of advertisers, picketing, loading of a newspaper's mail to the point where it is unmanageable, jamming classified advertising telephone lines, and telephoned midnight threats of bodily harm to publishers, editors and their families."

Late in 1965, there began to be evidence that Birchers and other Radical Rightists in California were buying suburban dailies and weeklies, and shopping news "throwaways," in what appeared to be the beginning of an effort to build a Birchite Radical Rightist press network in the myriad California suburbs. In mid-1965, for example, the Downey, Calif., *Live Wire* was sold to a group that included a John Birch Society coordinator.

The Police Question

One of the most persistent Birch Society campaigns of the last few years—and to some, one of the more alarming ones—is wrapped up in the Birch slogan, "Support Your Local Police." It is both a part of the national Birch program and an intensive local activity; it involves infiltration and it makes use of front groups; it is a holding maneuver against the enemy, a Society recruiting device, a propaganda slogan, and a hullabaloo of buttons and bumper-stickers.

The campaign, begun originally in the Society's *Bulletin* of July, 1963, was obviously designed to exploit the so-called white backlash and to win friends for Welch's movement—and more particularly, to draw recruits wearing blue uniforms into the Birch chapters.

As it began, Welch declared policemen to be "the best friends everywhere of anti-Communists, like ourselves." The question that immediately arose stemmed from the Welch-Birch view of all-pervading Communism in American life. Just how would friendship with the Birch sort of *"anti*-Communist" affect the required neutrality and objectivity of law enforcement officers? For example, with respect to police handling of civil rights problems? The Birch drive had been kicked off in that first *Bulletin* with a paragraph of generous praise for the handling of Negro demonstrations by the police of Birmingham, Ala.—including their use of police dogs against peaceful demonstrators.

Within a year, hundreds of Committees to Support Your Local Police were established in communities all over the country. They have since distributed literally tons of Society literature and served as recruitment teams.

Through such local efforts the Birch Society has enlisted, according to publicity chief Rousselot, a "growing number of police and personnel in sheriffs' departments throughout the country." Such recruitment has been pressed vigorously; in many cities its success, and the possibilities of police-Birch alliances, have become matters of deep concern.

177

In Santa Ana, Calif.—a city of 100,000 lying 30 miles southeast of Los Angeles—the membership of the Birch Society's Chapter QXTZ was composed of 23 city police officers. A private detective, assigned by the city manager to investigate a mysterious campaign of harassment against Police Chief Edward Allen (such as anonymous telephone calls at night; an unsigned pamphlet questioning his honesty; the theft of his badges at headquarters and false alarms that dispatched fire trucks to his home), reported that the incidents had been perpetrated by members of QXTZ as a power play to get rid of a chief they did not like.

The John Birch chapter controlled the Santa Ana Police Benevolent Association, all of its officials but one being QXTZ members, and under this controlling majority the PBA by-laws were changed to enable a grievance committee to hear secret testimony against Chief Allen. One lieutenant was later dismissed from the force for engaging in Birch recruiting while on duty and for misappropriating a police vehicle. He allegedly used it while on a secret snooping mission aimed at discrediting the chief.

Other communities have witnessed what may be the beginning of a process that tears at departmental loyalties and community unity. For example:

• Two police officers in Minneapolis, one of them a deputy inspector, openly criticized the nation's courts in addresses delivered before a meeting of Birch Society members.

• In Salisbury, Mass., all persons attending the 1965 Police Association banquet on June 23 were given copies of a "Support Your Local Police" pamphlet published by the Birch Society.

• In Jersey City, N.J., in April, 1966, a policeman was charged with using police pouches to distribute John Birch Society literature to colleagues. Police spokesmen, in halting the distribution, denied that it had been done under official auspices.

• The police chief of Trenton, N.J., quoted the Society's monthly *Bulletin* verbatim in a departmental memo sent to all his men.

• In Las Vegas, Nev., in September, 1966, more than a hundred police and sheriff's officers viewed screenings of a Birchite propaganda film, *Anarchy, U.S.A.,* which purports to show a Communist conspiracy behind the civil rights movement. At the same time, the Chairman of the Nevada Equal Rights Commission said that for some months he had been receiving reports of a Birchite attempt to infiltrate the local law enforcement agencies.

• James J. Allman, director of community relations for the St. Louis Police Department, resigned his position to become the Birch Society's paid coordinator for the state of Missouri.

• In New Jersey, State Trooper George Demetry resigned from the force to take a full-time job as a Society organizer. The State Police Superintendent said that a conference with Demetry indicated the trooper had allowed his personal philosophy to influence his professional behavior.

• In Newark, N.J., a policeman was given a three-month leave of absence to conduct Birch recruiting activities. He later went to work permanently as a Society coordinator.

• In Los Angeles, Rousselot claimed, in the fall of 1965, that at least three district attorney's investigators, more than 25 policemen, about 15 sheriff's deputies and other law enforcement personnel were members of the Society.

• In Massachusetts, in March, 1966, members of the Birch Society were urged by the group's New England regional director to work for the defeat of proposed legislation that would establish civilian police review boards in the Commonwealth. As a result, the chairman of the legislative committee dealing with the bill was "flooded" with mail in opposition to the measure. The bill was defeated the following month.

• Official Birch material has been placed on the police

bulletin board in Rockford, Ill., and on at least one precinct bulletin board in New York City.

• A large number of city policemen attended a rally at New York's Town Hall auditorium in July, 1965; the rally was sponsored by the Birch Society's American Opinion Speakers Bureau. A New York *Post* reporter judged that the officers, identifiable by their Patrolmen's Benevolent Association lapel buttons, made up a majority of the audience. One of the speakers, a Birch Society Section Leader, declared: "Some people hate the police. The Birch Society has the answer—it is the only hope for the world."

New York's Finest

The issue of Birchism among New York policemen arose preceding the 1964 elections when manifestations of the Society's propaganda were noted on police short-wave radio conversations. As an aftermath, the Police Commissioner ordered a departmental investigation to determine whether the Birch Society could be considered a "political" organization falling within the prohibition of existing departmental rules and whether membership in the Society would be inconsistent with service on the police force. The results of the investigation were never made public.

In May, 1966, after holding hearings, a joint New York State legislative committee on election and corporation laws declared that the Birch Society, in its opinion, was a political organization and that any policeman who belonged to it violated the Penal Law. Subsequently, however, the New York Police Commissioner was advised by the City's Corporation Counsel that prohibition by him of police membership in the Birch Society "would appear to be an unwarranted interference of the constitutional right of association."

The Police Commissioner, Howard R. Leary, who earlier said that he was "repelled and nauseated" by many of the Society's views, stated that Birchers on the force would be judged, and promoted, solely on their actions as policemen. He said that passage of legislation banning Birch membership on the city's police force would aid him greatly. He added that if he had the authority, he would not allow policemen to join the Society.

Significantly, more than a handful of "Support Your Local Police" committees have been established in New York City either by Birch members or by others closely identified with Society members and their goals. Their primary activity during 1966 was directed toward opposing the establishment—and subsequently the maintenance—of a civilian-controlled police complaint review board.

Such a board began functioning with apparent success in the city in July, 1966. But it was short-lived as a result of its defeat in a city-wide referendum placed on the Election Day, 1966, ballot by the local Patrolmen's Benevolent Association. Police Commisioner Leary supported the board, which, he said, "has certainly strengthened the spirit of cooperation between the police and the public."

In an unsuccessful pre-election attempt to save the city's civilian complaint review board, New York's United States Senators, Republican Jacob K. Javits and Democrat Robert F. Kennedy, jointly made known the active role of the Birch Society and its members in the anti-review board effort and declared their belief that the Society would use the campaign to broaden its influence both locally and nationally. The Javits-Kennedy statement on the activity of the Birchers in the campaign to eliminate the civilian-controlled review board was largely based on a report prepared at their request by the Anti-Defamation League of B'nai B'rith.

The ADL report included the following information:
• The Birch Society has long called on members to "oppose the formation or continuance of police review boards." As far back as July, 1963, the Society *Bulletin* ordered members to work against review boards. The August, 1964, *Bulletin* stated:

181

"Oppose the establishment of 'police review boards' in your cities, towns, or local communities, no matter what excuses and propaganda are advanced in their support. Not all policemen are angels, but all Communists *are* devils —and we're on the side of the angels."

• The Society's first major "Support Your Local Police" effort in New York City occurred in 1965—at the time that the proposal to set up a civilian review board was under consideration. In May, 1965, a "special project of the day" undertaken by all Birch Society chapters throughout New York was an all-out campaign to gather signatures on petitions opposing a civilian review board. Birchers dutifully carried out their orders, collecting thousands of signatures on such petitions from their fellow New Yorkers.

The 1965 petitions, which did not bear the name of the Society itself, carried the names of Birch front groups. They were limited to expressing support for the New York City police and opposing a civilian review board. Unwary citizens signing the petitions were told merely that their signatures would be presented to the Mayor or the City Council. In short, a classic example of the use of front groups to exploit an issue for Birchite purposes.

• In July, 1966, just after creation of the civilian review board, the Birch Society furnished foot soldiers for the forces seeking to overthrow the board at a referendum in November, 1966. Society members were actively involved in the petition campaign by the Patrolmen's Benevolent Association to put the issue on the ballot. The Society distributed PBA petitions to its members and urged them to gather signatures.

The effort to eliminate the review board in the referendum became the top priority project of Birch chapters in New York. And to make certain that their total effort was concentrated on the fight, those chapters put aside other projects until after Election Day, devoting all their efforts to the distribution of "Support Your Local Police," TACT, PBA and other anti-review board material. The Birchers formed only a small segment of the anti-board forces—but were among the most zealous.

Significantly, at the time the Society was marshaling all its resources in New York for the drive, it was attempting to hide its true role from the public by distributing its propaganda through front groups.

Nevertheless, there was little doubt that the ultimate goal of the Society was the expansion of its own membership. Indeed, Welch had stated in the November, 1965, *Bulletin:*

> In the course, therefore, of discovering the surprising truth about the charges of police brutality, the real significance of the clamor for police review boards, and all other aspects of the campaign to discredit and demoralize local police forces, [the] ordinary good citizen can be led into a realization of the truth about a lot of other things. So that our campaign, *Support Your Local Police,* becomes not only more and more valuable and meaningful for its direct and specific purpose, but extremely helpful as a part of our total educational program.

Welch later gloated in the June, 1966, *Bulletin:*

"In this undertaking our success has greatly outrun our 'fame.' For probably two-thirds of the people in the United States who are now giving their moral backing to *Support Your Local Police* campaigns do not have any idea that this began as, and still is, a John Birch Society project. Which is all right with us."

In an obvious attempt to win additional support from members of the police, the Birch Society in 1965 established a committee called the Police Award Reserve (PAR). Operating out of Society headquarters in Belmont, and under the chairmanship of Birch National Executive Council member Laurence E. Bunker, this so-called "independent committee" seeks to provide "posthumous honor and recognition" to policemen killed performing their duty.

The Danger

The danger in Birchite influence in the field of law enforcement is the Society's view of American law itself: it preaches that much of existing law is unconstitutional and perhaps even subversive, and that the courts of the country are serving a Communist conspiracy.

Still another danger lies in the possible manipulation of the police power itself by a quasi-political force that subscribes to a strange, extremist creed and whose members take direction from a leader who controls their monolithic organization. Most important is the fact that membership in The John Birch Society (like membership in the Communist Party) is not open and above-board. It is most often secret—which means that local police departments cannot know whether any particular officer is a Society member, and whether he may therefore have divided loyalties.

Commenting on police membership in the Birch Society, Mayor James H. J. Tate of Philadelphia, Pa., remarked: "This is the way the Nazi Party began."

Though the Society has apparently had only limited success in infiltration so far, the value of the "Support Your Local Police" campaign for purposes of public image, and as an aid in general recruiting, should not be underestimated.

The real significance of the campaign, however, lies perhaps in its implication for the civil rights movement. For Welch began it—at least in the pages of the Birch Society *Bulletin*—with the situation in Birmingham, where the police and civil rights workers were clearly squared off against each other. The implication was that civil rights activity was a *lawless* cause, quite aside from the usual Birch charge that it is controlled by Communists.

CHAPTER THIRTEEN

Public Relations

In the period of its rapid membership growth that began in 1964, the Society began to use modern public relations techniques to try to change its public image. It sought to lose some of the flavor of secrecy and irresponsible extremism and to develop an aura of respectability. It tried to portray itself as a group of conservative, patriotic citizens, dedicated to saving the Republic from the Communist influences it sees as pervading all aspects of American life—allegedly aided and abetted by five Presidents, by cabinet members, judges, and other national leaders.

Senator Goldwater's defense of extremism at the 1964 Republican National Convention helped start the image change, giving to the Radical Right a degree of respectability that aided their growth in the months that followed. The former Senator has since been critical of the Society.

The very same summer that saw Mr. Goldwater nominated for President also brought a major effort on the part of the Society to improve its public image—the establishment of its own Public Relations Department.

To head the campaign, Welch chose former Rep. John H. Rousselot, a California Republican and a personable public relations man. He had served for almost two years as the Society's Western States "Governor" following his 1962 defeat in a bid for re-election to Congress as one of the two known Birchers in the lower House.

Rousselot, whose *Beliefs and Principles of The John Birch Society*—after being entered into the *Congressional Record*—became a standard Society leaflet, was assisted by several Regional Public Relations Managers, based in strategic locations around the country.

Rousselot's headquarters in San Marino, Calif., a wealthy Los Angeles suburb, also served as the headquarters for all Society operations in the Far West.

Birch Society public relations has ranged from the sublime—a colorful and thoroughly professional Sunday supplement, published in major newspapers as a Birch ad —to the ridiculous, the last digits of the Society's telephone number at its Washington office being "1984."

The Birch Sunday Supplement

The expensive, multicolored 16-page Sunday supplement was Rousselot's first major project as Public Relations Director of the Society. Printed by rotogravure with negatives supplied by Birch headquarters itself, the supplement soft-pedaled Welch's wild charges against President Eisenhower and other American leaders of the last three decades. Ignoring the more extreme Birch positions on public affairs, the supplement portrayed the Society as a polished, responsible, advisory council of dedicated, prominent, patriotic citizens of conservative viewpoint whose only aim is to fight Communism and restore high moral, civic and religious idealism to America.

While the supplement was written by the Society's headquarters under Rousselot's supervision, it was printed locally and the cost in each city was borne by local Birch members and wealthy supporters, who often made their contributions anonymously.

The supplement first appeared in September, 1964, in the Los Angeles *Times* and the Los Angeles *Herald Examiner*. The cost was about $75,000. An additional $25,000 reportedly was spent on radio and other promotion—a total cost of almost $100,000, contributed by a wealthy Californian.

The supplement was placed in some 16 leading newspapers such as the Chicago *Tribune,* the Detroit *Free Press,* the Boston *Herald* (which gave the proceeds to charity while criticizing the Society), the Pittsburgh *Press,* the St. Louis *Globe-Democrat,* the Milwaukee *Journal,* the Indianapolis *Times,* and the Dallas *Morning News.* In Houston, copies of the supplement were mailed directly to individual homes, addressed merely to "Occupant."

In its effort to create a more respectable image, one page in the supplement carried photographs of well-known Americans, quoting each in a few good words for the Birch organization. Included were Sen. Strom Thurmond (R., S.C.); Tom Anderson, a member of the Society's own National Council; Rev. J. L. Ward, a Negro Birch ally; and former Secretary of Agriculture Ezra Taft Benson, who served in the Eisenhower Cabinet and whose son, Reed, is the Society's Washington, D.C., representative.

On the following page there appeared the picture and a laudatory quote from an "ordinary" member—the only one so honored. She was identified as Mrs. Beth Cleminson of San Gabriel, Calif., who explained in the quotation why she joined the Society. Persons who have corresponded with the Society's office in San Marino, Calif., recognized Mrs. Cleminson's name. She was secretary to Rousselot.

Indicative of the techniques employed in the Society's public relations project was the use—in the original Los Angeles version of the supplement—of a picture of Dwight Eisenhower accompanied by a quotation apparently praising The John Birch Society. Welch's characterization of General Eisenhower as "a dedicated, conscious agent of the Communist conspiracy" was by that time a matter of public knowledge all across the country. The former President's public expression of distaste for the Society, and its attempt to use his name, forced a change in the supplement. All reference to him was deleted. Said Eisenhower:

I have no respect whatsoever for that individual or for anyone else who associates himself with such unconscionable practices.

Welch's charge that President Eisenhower was an agent of Communism has been one of the most serious problems that has faced the Society—a fact admitted by East Coast Public Relations Manager Thomas Davis after he resigned at the end of 1966. It has caused considerable chagrin to the Society's constituency, some of whom have stated publicly that they do not agree on that point with the man whose leadership they follow dutifully and who runs the Society with a firm hand.

Rousselot was quoted in the Sacramento *Bee* of April 11, 1965, as declaring that Welch had been right about Eisenhower. On the other hand, Rousselot tried to disassociate the Society from the extremist views of Welch on the subject of President Eisenhower, Milton Eisenhower, the late John Foster Dulles, and ex-CIA Chief Allen Dulles, all of whom were branded as agents of Communism by Welch in his notorious book, *The Politician.*

In a June 22, 1965, press release, Rousselot quoted Welch as stating:

"Neither The John Birch Society nor its members have ever had any connection with *The Politician* in any way. . . ."

The statement was less than completely candid. *The Politician,* expurgated, has received widespread distribution through the organized efforts of Society officials and Society members ever since Welch published it. The cleansed version that appeared in early 1963 contained softer language about President Eisenhower. But it did not alter the basic thrust that the former President was a Communist agent. (Society members were never explicitly told that the published version differed in its text from the original, although an explanation was included in the revised text. Instead they—and the public—were told to "Read It and Judge For

Yourself"—as if the readers were getting the original version.)

Not only have individual Birchers been active in distributing *The Politician*. It is sold in every American Opinion bookstore. It has been advertised in Birch Society publications. It is lent to new members by the chapters, each of which receives a free copy. It has been recommended in the Birch *Bulletin* as a tool for recruiting, and has been promoted at Birch meetings and rallies.

A Measure of Success

Despite Welch's extremist enormities, the Society had a minor measure of success in its efforts to improve its image and achieve a degree of respectability. Rousselot, Davis, Reed Benson, and the other public relations men —clean-cut, conservative-looking, button-down-shirt types— made themselves more easily accessible and available to the press, to radio and to TV. When they were able to expound dedicated patriotism and anti-Communism without having to cope with the problem of Welch's extremism, they came across to the average listener as mere conservatives. When pressed, however, they were prisoners of the real Birch line that the nation is well down the road to Communism and that the whole American society is heavily infested with Communistic influences.

A stable of Birchite speakers has brought the Birch line to college campuses, local civic associations, service clubs and veterans' organizations. The Birchers take booths at state and county fairs. Local chapters have entered patriotic floats in many a holiday parade; some have even won prizes. The public relations benefits to the Society are obvious.

In at least one California community, the Chamber of Commerce has listed the Birch cell as a recognized community organization. When an American Opinion bookstore was opened during 1965 in a Milwaukee suburb, its

Mayor personally cut the tape at a formal ceremony attended by Welch.

Yet the Society remains trapped, in its efforts to build a better image, by its own extremism. When Reed Benson opened the Washington, D.C., office in September, 1965, reporters asked whether he thought President Johnson to be guilty of treasonable acts. Benson replied:

"The Constitution defines treason as giving aid and comfort to the enemy, and I believe we are giving aid and comfort to the enemy. What do you call it?"

On the Air

Although Robert Welch has remained steadfast in his faith in the "printed word," he announced in January, 1966, that the Birch Society would take a fling at radio broadcasting—the chief propaganda medium of the non-Birch Radical Right. The Society launched a weekly, 15-minute radio program called The Birch Report. Welch explained to his members that the time had come when, "with our emphasis on the printed word still unabated, we need at least a limited but periodical use of the broadcasting media, even if for no other reason than the direct purposes of our Public Relations Department." Rousselot was to supervise the program, which would be paid for by multiple local sponsorship. "In plain language," Welch said, "we are counting on our members throughout the country, especially those with businesses that can use local radio advertising to advantage, to sponsor this program in their respective areas."

The Birch Report, featuring talks by leading Society spokesmen and occasional invited guests, is taped and mailed to sponsors or stations for $5 per broadcast. The response of members who have become commercial sponsors has been gratifying to Welch. The first broadcast was sent out in the second week in February, 1966, and within a month it was being heard on 70 stations across the country.

By April there were 79 stations on the Birch network, by May, over a hundred. In July there were 148, and by October, 176. The Birch Society was challenging Hargis, Smoot, and McIntire in their own field, and as "public relations" it was a potent weapon.

An Embarrassing Episode

Toward the end of 1965, the Birch Society was confronted with an embarrassing public relations problem—right in its own New England back yard. A local Birch leader in Middleboro, Mass., inserted an ad in a local paper, announcing a Society meeting. The ad quoted six lines from a letter written some years ago by Richard Cardinal Cushing of Boston in which he had praised Welch and endorsed the Society—a letter whose content the Cardinal had later repudiated.

When Cardinal Cushing learned that his old letter was again being used by Birch Society members, he wrote Welch to protest:

> It is happening again and again. Your field agents . . . use a letter I sent years ago. . . .
> What am I to do with regard to having my name misused in this fashion? You know that I have absolutely nothing to do with the John Birch Society—I was never a member of it and I simply cannot understand the means this organization uses in recruiting members. . . .
> If I had had this ad in my hands last Saturday, I would have had every Catholic Church in the neighborhood announce on the following day that they were to disregard this publicity in its entirety and at the same time advise the Catholic people that I have no respect for or confidence in those behind the Middleboro Branch of the John Birch Society.
> I have yet to find a member of the Society whom I would trust as a result of the way its leaders have used a letter I sent years ago to some one in California in which I paid you a high personal tribute. What a fool I was

191

to put in writing my one time admiration and affection for you.

Leo Kahian, the Middleboro Birch leader responsible for the ad, said later he had made a mistake in quoting the old letter by the Cardinal and that he had not known that the Society warned all chapters in May, 1964, not to use it.

The Boston Sunday *Herald* reported that Welch had sent a letter of apology to Cardinal Cushing, but the publication in the same paper of the Cardinal's sharp letter to Welch did nothing to enhance the Society's image in the heavily Catholic areas of New England.

Public Relations and Recruiting

Exactly where the Society's public relations program was headed seemed an open question early in 1967. The resignations of Rousselot and Davis, the two best-known public relations executives in the Society's stable, certainly seemed to signal the end of an era—the end of the first sustained effort by the Society to polish up its public image.

There had been some successes—but the public relations campaign headed for more than two years by Rousselot had failed in its basic and primary goal: it had failed to wipe out the public view of the Birch Society as a radical, extremist, and irresponsible organization, given to reckless charges and beset by a fantasy-world view of the United States and the world.

Many responsible leaders of the Republican Party had rejected and repudiated the Society. So had such leading conservatives as former Senator Goldwater and *National Review* editor William F. Buckley, Jr.

Despite the basic failure of the Birchite public relations effort in its first two years, there was no indication that the Society itself was any worse off than when the program was launched in the summer of 1964—and in fact the organization had grown and expanded in that time.

Public relations techniques were an aid to Birch Society

recruiting, but they were not—and they are not—a substitute for the actual, continuing, hard-nosed recruiting program being carried out by the Society. The 75 or 80 coordinators in the field, backstopped by a headquarters team that supervises various geographical areas of the country, are the heart of the Birchite organizing apparatus. They are the key to keeping existing chapters to the Birch line and working full blast on Society projects, and to organizing new chapters as well.

It costs the Society roughly $15,000 to put a new coordinator into the field, including his first year's salary and the books and equipment he needs, such as films, projectors, and tape recorders. The 30 or 35 coordinators added to the Society's staff during the last two years or so represented an investment by the Birch organization of roughly half-a-million dollars. To put new salesmen into the field requires a steady and growing reservoir of capital to sustain them during training and the initial period of work—until they organize enough new chapters to achieve a kind of self-supporting status through the dollar inflow that new members supply. That is why Welch, Rousselot, and the Society's professional staff, aided by National Council members and key supporters across the country, have devoted a major portion of their time to fund-raising.

Throughout 1966, as in the preceding years, members and friends of The John Birch Society received written fund-raising appeals from Welch and from the Society's Executive Committee. Stressing the theme that only the Society barred the way to a Communist takeover of the United States, a May appeal called on Birchers to join a "Continuing Century Club"—an extension of a Welchian plan whereby a contributor pledged to give the Society $100 a month for a period of three years.

A few months later, in July, 1966, Welch broadened the "club plan" to include The Sawbuck Club for those who would pledge $10 a month; The Quarter-Century Club for $25 givers; The Half-Century Club—$50 monthly; The Century Club—$100; The Big D Club—$500; and The Millennium Club—$1,000 a month.

In September, an eight-page fund-raising appeal, entitled *Full Speed Ahead,* was sent out over the signatures of the Society's Executive Committee, headed by Milwaukee industrialist William J. Grede (who also heads the heavily Birch-flavored, politically oriented 1976 Committee). It sought contributions of $1,000—at once.

The extra-frequent fund-raising appeals in May, July, August and September, 1966, appeared by year's end to have accomplished their purpose. There were clear signs that the Birch Society had surmounted the cash-bind which had appeared to plague it earlier in the year.

If the membership growth rate had levelled off during 1966, it was at the same time clear that the Society could still mobilize the financial wherewithal to carry forward its activities and to point toward 1968 when the political atmosphere might again be ripe for expanded propaganda and recruitment efforts.

CHAPTER FOURTEEN

The Birch Map

By the end of 1966, the 4,000 chapters of The John Birch Society sprawled from coast to coast, and from the Gulf Coast to the Canadian border, with units in Alaska and members in Hawaii as well.

The total membership was in the range of 75,000 to 85,000, despite well-publicized claims by Society spokesmen during 1966 that the membership had reached the 100,000 mark—and one or two enthusiastic coordinators even claimed more than 100,000.

Perhaps 50,000 to 60,000 of the Birch faithful were embraced in the 4,000 chapters. The rest, perhaps one-fourth to one-third of the total, held membership in the so-called "Home Chapter." This is a catch-all designation that includes several different types of members who do not participate in local chapter activities in their own communities, but who receive their monthly *Bulletins* and other materials direct from Belmont.

The "Home Chapter" includes members who do not wish to risk any identification with the Society in their own communities or anywhere else. These are often some of the wealthiest and most influential supporters of the Birch group. The "Home Chapter" also includes members who have moved, and have therefore dropped out of their old local chapters, but have not settled in a new location where they can join a new local chapter. Finally, "Home

Chapter" status is often assigned to laggard members who do not attend local chapter meetings regularly, who are delinquent in their dues, or who have been troublemakers in their local units. For the latter group, "Home Chapter" status is often the final way station before the Society drops them from membership—or before they quit.

During the latter part of 1965 and throughout 1966, Society chapters in some parts of the country appeared to be undergoing a process of consolidation, with weak and inactive chapters being disbanded or merged with stronger and more active units. It appeared that a conscious effort was being made by the top leadership of the Society to trim away excess fat and deadwood—the overgrowth that took place in the wake of the Society's rapid growth during the 1964 election campaign and immediately thereafter.

In large measure, this process of trimming the Society to a leaner and more streamlined silhouette accounts for the apparent decline in the number of Birch chapters from an estimated 5,000 to 4,000. The decline in chapters does not necessarily reflect a proportionate loss of membership, since many of those whose chapters were disbanded assumed "Home Chapter" status and continued as Birch members, or were transferred to other local chapters.

The Highlights

California, which has 17 full-time coordinators, continues to lead the nation in Birchite strength, with some 12,000 to 15,000 members organized in 1,000 to 1,200 chapters. The Society scored some gains in Northern California, where recruiting had lagged, and by the end of 1966 boasted some 3,000 members there. The rest were concentrated in Southern California—the strongest Birch area in the nation. The bulk of this concentration was in Greater Los Angeles, with perhaps 3,000 members in adjacent Orange County, and another thousand in the San

Diego area, which has five American Opinion bookstores.

The Birch Society's strength in California, especially in the conglomeration of suburbs in Southern California, underscores what has long been apparent to students and observers of the Birch manifestation in the United States of the 1960s: that the Society is a middle-class movement, composed largely of white-collar and professional people, and that it finds its most ready reservoir of support in the suburbs.

Recruitment in the big cities and metropolitan centers has never been easy or successful for the Society, but once its coordinators move ten, fifteen, or twenty miles out of town—to the suburban communities that sometimes serve as "bedroom" communities for those who commute to the cities—they meet with far greater success.

Besides California, other areas of high Birch concentration dot the country—clustered around major cities, but generally not in them. In the South, Birmingham, Ala., Atlanta, Ga., and Miami, Fla., are strong points. In the Southwest, Houston, Dallas-Fort Worth, San Antonio, and Amarillo, Texas show some strength, and the Phoenix area in Arizona has emerged as a new citadel of Birchism.

The State of Washington is especially strong in the Pacific Northwest, with clumps of Birch strength in the Seattle and Spokane areas and perhaps 100 chapters elsewhere in the State.

Birchite pockets of concentration are scattered across America's Mid-Western heartland. Wichita, Kans., home of two members of the Society's National Council, has for some years been a strong point. In Wisconsin, Milwaukee and the suburbs strung out north of it, along Lake Michigan, are well-salted with Society activists, and just to the south, the suburbs above Chicago show considerable activity. Indianapolis, Evansville, and Fort Wayne are the Hoosier strong points, while Kansas City, Omaha, and St. Louis lead the way along the Missouri and Mississippi Rivers.

In the Rocky Mountain States, Denver has lagged compared to earlier years, but Salt Lake City appears to have shown Birchite gains.

In the East, the suburban pattern is obvious. The Birch Society has a pocket of strength in the communities clustered around Philadelphia. The same is true in New Jersey—a state that is largely suburban and in which the Society showed rapid growth in 1964 and 1965. In the New York area, suburban Long Island is the main center of strength, with lesser penetration in Westchester and other counties north and northwest of the metropolis.

New England, despite the location of the Society's national headquarters at Belmont, just outside of Boston, has never developed into a Birchite strong point. There is, nevertheless, noticeable activity in Connecticut, which has some 65 or 70 chapters, in southeastern Massachusetts, Cape Cod, and a few of the Boston suburbs, plus Nashua, N.H., where the Society has a cadre of active and zealous members.

Maine and Vermont, truly conservative in the best sense, have steadfastly rejected Birchite radicalism despite recruitment efforts that have sought to make a dent there since the Society was formed eight years ago.

State-by-State

Estimating Birch Society strength is a difficult business at best because membership figures remain, to this day, perhaps the most closely guarded Birch Society secret. Close study, however, makes possible some general estimates.

The South: In addition to the heavy Birch concentration around Birmingham, the Society in Alabama has strength in the Mobile area, around Montgomery, and in the Selma and Huntsville regions. In Arkansas, there is moderate strength in the Little Rock area and gains have been scored in Pine Bluff and Jonesboro. In Georgia, the Society has added a second coordinator, boasts well over

50 chapters in Atlanta, has a strong and active unit in Americus, and may hold a statewide membership total of perhaps 1,500. In Florida, there are possibly 1,000 members in Dade County, including greater Miami, with perhaps another 1,000 or so in the rest of southern Florida, clustered in the Tampa-St. Petersburg area, Sarasota (home of the pro-Birch Let Freedom Ring operation); in northern Florida, there are pockets of strength in Jacksonville, St. Augustine and Tallahassee. Three coordinators service the state. The Society has some strength in New Orleans and Shreveport, La., has scored gains in Mississippi, where the White Citizens' Councils are no longer so strong as they were ten years ago, but it appears to be lagging in the Carolinas. There is some Birchite strength in Virginia around Richmond and active units in northern Virginia, the District of Columbia, and Washington's Maryland suburbs. In Tennessee—home, like Kansas, of two Society National Councilors, Tom Anderson and A. G. Heinsohn, Jr.—big gains have been claimed by the resident Society coordinator.

The Southwest: Arizona, today one of the strongest Birchite states, has approximately 2,000 members, half of them in the Greater Phoenix area, several hundred more in Tucson, and the rest scattered around the state. Arizona is served by four full-time coordinators and in relation to its statewide population, ranks among the first five or six Birchite states. New Mexico has perhaps 400 members. Recruiting does not seem to have progressed very far in Oklahoma. As for Texas, the big, sprawling state is served by six or seven coordinators and may have several thousand members—but the Lone Star State Birchers have shown a tendency to go off on tangents not directly related to the Society's prescribed agenda of activity. Nevertheless, Texas Birchers are active in politics in some areas and are potentially a troublesome force.

The Far West: Other than California, the Society's strength in the Far West seems to be centered in the State of Washington, which has 1,000 members or more. There are only a few hundred members in Oregon, and clusters of strength in such Nevada population centers as Reno and Las Vegas. Alaska has eight or ten active chapters.

The Rocky Mountain States: Colorado and Wyoming appear to be stagnant states, but Birchers are somewhat more active in Montana—especially on the political front. Not much is heard of Birchite activity in Idaho, but there are functioning units there.

It is in Utah that the Society has made its strongest gains during the last year or so in a campaign that was obviously slanted at the heavily Mormon population in that state. In this the Society has had a generous assist from Ezra Taft Benson, a senior member of the Council of Twelve Apostles, ruling body of the Church of Latter-day Saints. Benson has, in the last year or so, made frequent speeches defending the Birch Society against its critics and praising the organization and its founder, Robert Welch—some of these speeches before Birch front groups. Benson reminds his audiences that he is not a member of the Society, but it is well known—to Mormons and to others—that his son, Reed, is a full-time paid executive of the Birch organization, with headquarters in Washington, D.C. Despite his Washington base, young Benson himself is a frequent speaker in heavily Mormon areas of the country—which include not only Utah, but Arizona, Idaho, Nevada, Wyoming, and Southern California as well. The identification of the Bensons with the Birch Society suggests the possibility of gains by the Society in those states during the months and years to come.

The Birch Society has made little effort to hide its obvious bid for Mormon support. A cover of *American Opinion* Magazine recently featured a full-color portrait of the late church leader J. Reuben Clark, Jr., who had been a member of the top governing body until his death in 1961. In April, 1966, during a Mormon Church con-

ference at Salt Lake City, a local Birch front group
scheduled Robert Welch at a $15 per plate dinner which
was attended by Apostle Benson, who had earlier been
billed to introduce Welch, but who, apparently, withdrew
because of some displeasure by certain church leaders.
Welch delivered an encomium to Benson, who received a
standing ovation from the audience.

At a news conference before the banquet, Welch met the
press beneath a large portrait of President David O. McKay,
beloved 92-year-old President of the Church of Latter-day
Saints. He declared openly:

> If we are looking for conservative, patriotic Americans
> of good character, humane consciences and religious
> ideals, where would you go looking for them any more
> hopefully than among the Latter-day Saints?
> The Latter-day Saints are as individuals the kind of
> people we would like to have in the John Birch Society.

The reported plan to have Benson introduce Welch
apparently led to an announcement by President McKay,
Hugh B. Brown, N. Eldon Tanner, and Joseph Fielding
Smith, who make up the First Presidency of the Mormon
Church, in which they declared that the church "is not
involved in this dinner in any way, and furthermore, that
the church has no connection with the John Birch Society
whatsoever."

Nevertheless, the Society has become eminently respectable in Utah and seeks to branch out and to boost its following in other Rocky Mountain and Western states where
Mormon influence is strong.

The Midwest: In addition to the areas of activity already
mentioned, the Society has been a factor on the Michigan
political scene for several years, causing problems for Gov.
George Romney and the state Republican organization.
The main center of Birch concentration is in the Greater
Detroit area. There is some Birch strength in Minnesota's

Twin Cities, and there are clumps of membership in Iowa and the Dakotas and well-scattered pockets of organization in Kansas and Nebraska.

Indiana has perhaps 1,000 Birch members in Indianapolis and two or three other cities. In Ohio, Birch activity has shown up in Cleveland, Toledo, Youngstown, and Cincinnati. Kentucky does not appear to be one of the stronger Society states. In Missouri, St. Louis is a main area of strength with perhaps 30 to 40 chapters and considerable Birchite front group activity. Aside from perhaps 30 chapters in northern Illinois, especially the Chicago suburbs, there is little Birch activity in the land of Lincoln and practically no activity downstate.

Wisconsin, with perhaps 1,000 to 1,500 members, is one of the strongest Birch states in mid-America.

The East: In Pennsylvania, the Society has added a new center of strength to its existing base in the Philadelphia area, scoring strong gains in the Pittsburgh area during the last year or two. New Jersey has perhaps 200 chapters and roughly 2,000 to 3,000 members, although there have been reports that the Garden State may have twice that strength. Despite New Jersey's emergence as a strong Birchite state during 1964 and 1965, there have not been any signs of great activity of the Society's followers—and if the seeds for future action have been sown, they do not appear to have sprouted yet.

New York State has several thousand Birch members, concentrated—as has been noted—in the Long Island area. Birch spokesmen have been quoted as saying there are 250 chapters—roughly 2,500 to 3,000 members—within a 50-mile radius of New York City, but that would include strength in northern New Jersey, Westchester, Long Island, and New York City itself.

Connecticut's 65 or 70 chapters are scattered in such communities as Stamford, Norwalk, Fairfield, Greenwich, Bridgeport, Stratford, New Haven, Danbury, Hartford, and Wethersfield.

Massachusetts has perhaps 40 to 50 chapters—possibly 1,000 members. There have been gains in the western part of the state. In Rhode Island, the Society has a half-dozen or a dozen chapters. Besides Nashua, New Hampshire has concentrations of Birchite activists in Manchester, Exeter, Derry, and several other communities—and they pepper the letters-to-the-editor columns of the Rightist *Union-Leader* in Manchester with an ongoing flow of Birchite "party line" messages. Letters to newspapers appear to be a favorite activity of New England Birchers.

Delaware and West Virginia do not appear to be centers of any noticeable Birch Society activity, and, as has been noted, Maine and Vermont are practically Birchite deserts.

CHAPTER FIFTEEN

The Apparatus

The staff and plant facilities of The John Birch Society have kept pace with the organization's membership growth over the years. The Society employs about 220 persons, including some 75 coordinators in the field, and meets a weekly payroll of approximately $40,000—more than $2 million a year.

At the beginning of 1967, Birch headquarters in Belmont could boast double the floor space it had in 1964—and what is more it had become the owner of its headquarters building, formerly rented, which was purchased during 1966 for some $330,000.

By 1966, the Society was spending well over $5 million a year. Though it apparently fell short of its 1966 income goal of $12 million, there was evidence that the Society was on much sounder financial ground in that year than it had been previously. Gone was the long series of testimonial dinners for Founder Welch that had been held in a number of cities during 1965 as a thinly disguised fund-raising operation and that, at $25 and $50 a plate, had raised almost a quarter-of-a-million dollars. In 1966, the Society appeared to be supporting itself comfortably—while spending at least $100,000 a week (its printing bill alone was some $125,000 a month).

The Complex

The national organization, which has already established itself as a unique apparatus on the usually-splintered Right, is a vast complex of local chapters, hierarchies, chains of command, public relations men, publishing companies, local organizations, discussion groups, fund-raisers, Red-hunters, bookstores, magazines, pressure groups, and movies for recruiting purposes.

Under the Birch Society's upper hierarchy—the founder, the Executive Committee, the National Council, and the coordinators—there exists a volunteer hierarchy of section and chapter leaders. Monthly, in the chapter leaders' homes, in quiet little cells of from 6 to 25 members (the average group is 10 or 15), the broad and busy base of the monolith meets.

Behind its efforts lies a corporate structure in which are found Robert Welch, Inc., The John Birch Society, Inc., the Belmont and Western Islands Publishing Companies, and the various enterprises bearing the name, "American Opinion."

There also exists a practical, energetic, and permanent apparatus for recruiting and for the production and marketing of propaganda, and a nationwide system of loosely organized but tightly orthodox front groups. There is a vast library of avowedly patriotic books, two Society-published magazines, a speakers' bureau, and hundreds of American Opinion bookstores.

The Magazine

American Opinion, the monthly magazine published by Robert Welch and The John Birch Society, selling for $1 a copy, is intended to be a molder of "Americanist" thinking, to instill in its readers a profound consciousness of the all-pervading Communist conspiracy allegedly stretching from the White House all the way down to the local town council, the school board, the public library, and the pulpit. The orthodoxy of the Society itself does not extend to *American Opinion;* its writers are given some latitude to express varying and sometimes contradictory opinions.

The latest official statement of *American Opinion*'s circulation and ownership was published in the December, 1966, issue. It showed an average press run for the year of 52,272 compared to 44,238 for 1965, or an increase of 18%. The average paid circulation for 1966 was 43,262, compared to 35,400 in 1965—an increase of 22%. The 1966 circulation was 70% higher than in 1964. The magazine has for several years sought to boost its newsstand distribution and sales, which are roughly half the paid circulation. Early in 1967, there were indications that these efforts were being intensified.

American Opinion magazine is owned by Robert Welch, Inc. Owners of 1% or more of the common stock in the corporation are The John Birch Society, Inc.; Miss Olive Simes of Boston; the Excelsior Housing Corp. of New York; Miss Ellen Lovett of Needham, Mass.; John Rousselot of Arcadia, Calif.; Thomas N. Hill of Gloucester, Mass.; Willard S. Voit of Balboa, Calif.; N. B. Hunt of Dallas, Tex.; and Rev. James Parker Dees of Statesville, N. C.

Robert Welch, Inc., is controlled by The John Birch Society, Inc., and has been ever since Welch gave his stock in Robert Welch, Inc., to the Society in 1960. The Society is a Massachusetts corporation of which Robert Welch himself is President. Miss Olive Simes is a wealthy Boston spinster who has for some time been a supporter of Birch activities and who, for many years, has been listed as a contributor to the Christian Nationalist Crusade, headed by Gerald Smith.

The Excelsior Housing Corp. is a South Carolina corporation that is a wholly owned subsidiary of Deering Milliken Inc., the well known textile firm. Miss Ellen Lovett is Robert Welch's long-time personal secretary. Rousselot has been Public Relations Director of the Birch Society, and Thomas N. Hill is Field Director of the Society.

Willard S. Voit is the official in charge of the Birch Society publications depot at Newport Beach, Calif. N. B. Hunt is a son of H. L. Hunt, the multi-millionaire whose fortune was amassed as an independent oil producer and who is the founder of the Far Rightist Life Line Foundation, Inc., propaganda operation, which conducts the Life Line broadcasts heard on some 400 radio stations.

Reverend Dees of Statesville, N.C., is an addition to the roster. He has been an official of the segregationist North Carolina Defenders of States' Rights, a member of the editorial advisory board of the Citizens' Councils of America magazine, and listed on the Liberty Lobby policy board.

Author James Graham Cook quotes Dees in his 1962 book, *The Segregationists,* as having stated: "I think Gerald L. K. Smith is the greatest patriot in this country today . . . He is a profound Christian. I know him personally, and I have a deep respect for him." According to Cook, Dees added: "I feel like there are good Jews and bad Jews; to Mr. Smith they're all bad . . . I've seen a lot of evidence that seems to substantiate his contentions."

Also in 1962, Smith described Dees as "our good friend and loyal supporter."

Robert Welch is the editor of *American Opinion,* the magazine he founded almost eleven years ago, which he formerly called *One Man's Opinion.* Scott Stanley, Jr., a young man active in Rightist causes before joining the magazine, is the managing editor. The associate editors are Thomas J. Anderson, a member of the Birch Society's National Council; Medford Evans, who is also an official of the White Citizens' Councils; Francis X. Gannon, the Society's research director; and E. Merrill Root, long a well known name in Rightist activities.

The contributing editors are Martin Dies, Sr., a former member of Congress from Texas who achieved national prominence as the head of the old Dies Committee, which investigated un-American activities in the 1930s and 1940s; Professor Hans Sennholz, an ex-Luftwaffe pilot who now teaches economics at Grove City (Pa.) College, an institution of higher learning heavily endowed by the Pew family who are principals in the Sun Oil Co. (J. Howard Pew, a leading supporter of Rightist causes in the United States, at one time served on the Editorial Advisory Committee of *American Opinion* magazine; Hilaire du Berrier, a foreign correspondent operating out of Paris, whose articles have frequently appeared in Rightist publications and who is author of the *H. du B. Reports;* Harold Lord Varney, leader of the Committee on Pan-American Policy, who has been active in Far Rightist causes for over thirty years; Robert H. Montgomery, a Boston lawyer who is a member of the Birch Society's National Council; and Frank Mac-Millan, who writes a monthly feature column in *American Opinion* called "From London."

Members of the magazine's 15-man Editorial Advisory Committee include Robert Dresser, a Providence, R.I., lawyer; Charles Edison, former Secretary of the Navy and Governor of New Jersey; J. Bracken Lee, former Governor of Utah; and Ludwig Von Mises, the prominent Austrian economist who is a leading prophet of nineteenth century laissez-faire economics; several members of the Society's National Council; and a few long-time Society sympathizers.

The Birch monthly is a glossy and well-written periodical, and is nurtured by advertisements, mostly from corporations that support the Far Right or in which Birch leaders have a substantial interest. These include the Allen-Bradley Co., of Milwaukee, which repeatedly purchases a multicolored back-page ad in *American Opinion;* the Rock Island Oil & Refining Co., Inc., of Wichita, whose principal is Fred Koch, a Society National Council member, and Spindale Mills, Spindale, N. C., in which Council member A. G. Heinsohn, Jr., is a principal.

Other advertising is purchased by organizations and publishing companies of the Far Right, and from time to time, by respected book publishers. But noteworthy is the substantial proportion of "house ads" trumpeting books published by Western Islands, the Birch publishing house.

On the cover of *American Opinion* each month, there shines forth a commercially slick portrait of an "Americanist" hero such as the late Syngman Rhee, the late Sen. Joseph McCarthy, or Ezra Taft Benson, or an *American Opinion* regular such as Martin Dies or novelist Taylor Caldwell.

American Opinion has, Welch hopes, some 80,000 salesmen—all members of the Birch Society—being constantly pressed to sell subscriptions and to persuade local newsstands and drugstores to stock a few copies each month. An offer is made of a handsome profit of 40¢-50¢ a copy, made possible by the magazine's high retail price.

Welch tries to shrug off Birch Society responsibility for the Society-controlled magazine whenever a writer runs to an embarrassing extreme. Welch claims he allows writers a sort of intellectual "freedom."

The Printed Word

Unlike many of the Society's allies on the Far Right—such as Billy James Hargis, Dan Smoot, Carl McIntire, H. L. Hunt and Clarence Manion—Robert Welch until recently put little faith in radio broadcasting for his "educational" programs. "From the very beginning," he wrote in the November, 1964, *Bulletin,* "we have depended on the surer, harder road of education through the printed word." And Welch's conviction is reflected in statistics:

The Society's printing bill is $1.5 million a year. It publishes and sells books with a retail value of more than $2 million annually.

Welch also publishes a new pocket-sized weekly, *Review of the News,* a magazine containing a day-by-day summary of world news without comment and with little slant, except in the choice of items. Presumably subscribers can use the magazine as a substitute for daily newspapers, which the Birch Society views as heavily penetrated by the Communist conspiracy anyway. *Review of the News* includes a section titled "Correction, Please!"—items in the news, followed by the editors' slanted answers to alleged "falsehoods, distortions, and more subtle Communist propaganda of infinite variety, in newspapers, magazines and over the air."

The latest official statement of *The Review of the News'* circulation and ownership was published in the issue for October 19, 1966. It disclosed that the average total distribution of the publication for the preceding 12 months had been 5,775 copies, and that 8,385 copies of the single issue nearest to the filing date had been distributed. *The Review of the News* is owned by Robert Welch; The John Birch Society, Inc.; and Miss Ellen Lovett, of Needham, Mass. Its editor is Scott Stanley, Jr., who is also managing editor of *American Opinion* magazine.

The publication's assistant editor is Founder Welch's wife, Marian Probert Welch; the news editors are James J. Drummey and Vincent J. Ryan, members of the JBS research staff; analysis editor is Samuel L. Blumenfeld; correction editor is Francis X. Gannon; business manager is Donald R. Gray; and circulation manager is George F. Edwards, Sr.

With book publishing a major activity in Belmont, the dollar-a-copy American Opinion Reprint Series has been replaced by The Americanist Library, glossy paperbacks published by Western Islands. The Americanist Library includes "One Dozen Candles," a group of books viewed by the Society as "Americanist" classics and as essential introductory reading for recruits or applicants.

An insight into the size of the publishing operation can be gained from the fact that the minimum printing of each title in the Americanist Library series is 100,000 copies.

Titles in the One Dozen Candles series indicate the

kind of required reading expected of Birch members before they are considered properly indoctrinated:

—*While You Slept,* by the late John T. Flynn.

—*Seeds of Treason,* by Ralph deToledano.

—*America's Retreat From Victory,* by the late Sen. Joseph R. McCarthy.

—*The Whole of Their Lives,* by the late Benjamin Gitlow, a Communist leader of the 1920s who broke with the CP.

—*Shanghai Conspiracy,* by retired Maj. Gen. Charles A. Willoughby, Gen. Douglas MacArthur's Intelligence chief in World War II, and a leading figure on the American Far Right.

—*From Major Jordan's Diaries,* by George Racey Jordan, which tells of the author's belief that American secrets were handed over to Soviet Russia during World War II.

—*I Saw Poland Betrayed,* by former Ambassador Arthur Bliss Lane—purporting to tell how American money, prestige, and productive might were used by the Communists to enslave Eastern Europe.

—*The People's Pottage,* by Garet Garrett on "the Communist-inspired conversion of America from a constitutional republic of self-reliant people into an unbridled democracy of handout-seeking whiners."

—*The Kohler Strike,* by Sylvester Petro—"the part played by labor bosses, whom the Communists love, in gradually destroying our great inheritance."

—*The Invisible Government,* by Dan Smoot, the story of the Council on Foreign Relations, which the Birchers claim is the "invisible government" seeking to convert the U. S. into a Socialist state, and then to make it a part of a one-world Communist system.

—*France, The Tragic Years,* by Sisley Huddleston—"de Gaulle's role in the Communist program," and "why the Communists and their allies appear to be the only stable group in French politics."

—Nine Men Against America, by Rosalie M. Gordon, described by the Birchers as "perhaps the most important on the list" because it claims to tell how the Supreme Court under Chief Justice Earl Warren has been "destroying every safeguard which might prevent the Communists from carrying out their plans" in the United States.

The Birch list of titles by Western Islands or other Birch publishing arms, plus books printed elsewhere but available through the Society, is a thick pamphlet. Besides "standards" of Far Right literature, the list includes some books by responsible conservatives, others by little-known extremists, and some legitimate classics such as works by John Stuart Mill, Adam Smith, and Frederic Bastiat. Included, too, are standard Birch Society documents—the Society's "introductory packet," one on civil rights, a "special" Society packet, and a "Warren Impeachment Packet."

Of interest also is the availability, through the Society, of the McGuffey Readers; a line of children's books series—Living American Stories, Childhood of Famous Americans Series, and Beginning-to-Read Books—all of which suggests that the Society is intent upon grooming a new generation of Birch moppets to carry on the fight years from now.

In the monthly *Bulletins,* Welch constantly and emphatically urges his members to read books. But it is important to note that it is his policy, and that of the Society, to tell them *exactly what books to read.* The "right" books are specifically prescribed in the *Bulletin* "agenda" and on *official* lists, and thus thousands of minds are neatly channeled into the straight and very, very narrow.

The Spoken Word

Because to a great many on the Far Right, hearing is believing, the Society has made audio-visual materials available and members are continually urged to start forums, lecture series, and study clubs. The following are relevant sections of that apparatus:

The American Opinion Speakers Bureau was started in 1962, and now offers Birch Society speakers such as Rousselot, Tom Anderson, Revilo Oliver, Reed Benson, and allies on the Far Right such as Harold Lord Varney, Willis Stone of the Liberty Amendment Committee, W. Cleon Skousen, and George Schuyler, the conservative Negro newspaper columnist, and former Sheriff Jim Clark of Selma, Ala.

Target organizations to which the services of these speakers are offered include not only Birch groups and fronts, but other Right Wing forums and, wherever possible, established civic, church, veterans, and school groups. Birchers are urged, when joining PTAs, political clubs and other community groups, to seek the position of program chairman to control the selection of speakers.

Speakers provided by the AOSB make about 100 appearances a month, addressing audiences at meetings from Nashua, N. H., to Pasadena, Calif.

The voices of Clarence Manion, Tom Anderson, and Welch, are familiar sounds at Birch meetings, study and discussion groups—via albums and tapes sold at Society bookstores. *One Dozen Trumpets* makes it possible for members to hear a full 18 hours of Founder Welch himself.

The Birch Bookstores

The John Birch Society has found it advantageous to establish its own outlets for published materials. Robert Welch's "reading rooms that sell books"—generally called American Opinion Bookstore, or American Opinion Library—have served as local headquarters for Right Wing books, flyers, films, rally tickets, and bumper stickers; as meeting places for Birch members, chapters and front groups; and as convenient recruiting depots for new members. The stores also serve in some places as local "stations" for Let Freedom Ring and as sponsors of the Society's radio program on local broadcasting outlets.

In 1963, there were about 100 of these shops; today there are about 350. They handle the standard Society materials as well as the output of Billy James Hargis, Dr. Fred Schwarz, Kent and Phoebe Courtney, the Circuit Riders, the Rev. Carl McIntire, Dan Smoot, and the Church League of America.

A development of recent years is the introduction of "mobile libraries"—Volkswagen buses which can be parked at street corners or outside Right Wing rallies. A New Yorker named Fred Lawrence, for example, has brought his book-laden VW into the Wall Street area to carry "the truth to the heathen," armed with Birch propaganda and a New York City peddler's license.

Robert Welch has been proud of his reading rooms, but Society officials sometimes deny their connection with the official apparatus when faced with embarrassment over the appearance of anti-Semitic materials in the stores or a revelation concerning an unsavory individual managing one. (In a Boston store in 1962, an associate of American Nazi Party leader George Rockwell managed the enterprise.)

Nevertheless, the connections between the individually owned bookstores and the Society itself are firm. The stores stock "recommended" materials, and many of these are ordered directly through Belmont headquarters—on credit. Robert Welch and John Rousselot have attended many a bookstore opening.

Carmine Saccardo, of Milford, Mass., a non-Bircher who took the "no-official-connection" claim seriously, told his story to reporter Bob Creamer of the Boston *Traveler*. Saccardo had taken over the ownership of Milford's Paul Revere Book Shop, and soon thereafter removed most of the Birch material from the shelves because it wasn't selling. Local Society members had tried to tell Saccardo what to order, and later boycotted his shop in protest against his displaying a picture of the late President Kennedy. Torn from his only market and saddled with a $4,000 debt, the well-meaning Saccardo closed up shop.

"My own friends were calling me a Communist," he declared, "and no matter what I said I couldn't make people understand."

Recruiting for Holy War

The John Birch Society is little interested in trying to understand the viewpoints of others. Birchers apparently find it more satisfying and less time-consuming to call them "Communists" and have done with it. The Society is quite energetic, however, in trying to make others understand *its* point of view.

As part of its overall and ongoing recruitment effort, the Society has in recent years produced several films suitable for "presentations." The first Birch presentation film featured Founder Welch in a two-and-a-half hour monologue condensing the Society's *Blue Book* into an overview of the vast, conspiratorial Communist-controlled world of which the United States was a part.

In 1965, at a cost of $70,000, the Society produced a second recruiting film relating the history, the aims and the operations of the Birch organization. It was intended as a companion piece to the Welch monologue—for prospects who had shown understanding of Birchism and serious interest in the Society. The second presentation, technically expert, asserts that while Americans were dancing (Fred Astaire was shown) and golfing (former President Eisenhower was shown), the Communist conspiracy was eating away at the foundations of the Republic. Then Robert Welch, the hero, decided to mobilize resistance into a vast patriotic organization. The operations of the Birch Society are then shown, from the headquarters in Belmont to the neighborhood chapter meeting.

In 1966, yet another recruitment film was produced, featuring Welch in a filmed version of his most recent summary of the conspiracy theory of history—the pamphlet called *The Truth in Time*.

215

After such films have been shown, Birch staffers deliver practiced pitches, urging those present to sign up as Society members. The Society has in recent years expected to sign up—sooner or later—about 25% of those who attend a presentation, but the leveling off of the membership growth rate during 1966 suggested that the pickings were becoming leaner and the hard sell harder.

Another device increasingly used in recent Birch Society recruiting drives is the newspaper advertisement. Birch Society ads are written and produced at headquarters in Belmont for placement by local Birch groups at their own expense. The ads, usually designed for a full page, appeal to good citizenship via the headline "Support Your Local Police"; to fear, via the message "What's Wrong With Civil Rights?," or to curiosity, via the caption "What Is The John Birch Society?—The Truth May Surprise You." The ads are usually a solid block of type.

The Society, however, has never solicited just *anyone* for membership. Welch seeks recruits with a potential for zeal, dedication, and indoctrination to serve as a cadre for missionary work at the grass roots. The films and the advertisements are aids to recruiting along with the specially designed recruiting packets. These have contained samples of Society literature, a copy of the Birch *Bulletin*, a copy of the Society's multicolored Sunday supplement—and, to be sure, an application for membership in the Society.

The formation of the AC Study Clubs mechanism appears—at least in part—to be a new recruiting device, perhaps dictated by the more recent difficulties in signing up new members. It is headed by Don Folkers, who devised the manual for the AC Study Clubs and who is headquartered at Belmont. The Society apparently hopes to lure prospective members into the fold by activating them through the clubs. The technique is reminiscent of the Marxist Study Clubs and study groups employed by the Communists in their recruiting efforts.

Whatever the device, whatever the technique, the Birch

Society improves each shining hour when it comes to recruiting new members—using the direct pitch, the front group, the study club, the printed word, the spoken word, the airwaves, modern public relations and advertising methods, and old-fashioned shoe leather. Its eyes are always on the distant goal—the day when it emerges as an organization more numerous and more powerful than it is at present, the day when it will flex its muscles, achieve political influence and power, and repeal what has been built up in twentieth century America of the last few decades.

Its day has not yet come, if it ever will, but even now, it is a large and formidable engine of propaganda and recruitment—a multimillion-dollar-a-year operation that is definitely a going concern.

CHAPTER SIXTEEN

Conclusions

We live in an age of extremism—an era which has spawned extremist manifestations in many areas of our national life. The last few years have seen the emergence of so-called pop art, the theater of the absurd, pornography that is palmed off as literature, the mod style and the mini-skirt in fashion, beards and beatniks in our cities, and cultists who preach the use of hallucinogenic drugs to expand individual consciousness. In the name of free speech, some young people have demonstrated for the right to use four-letter words.

In a time which has cast up every manner of extremist debris on our social shore, the question inevitably arises: Why is the political extremism of the Radical Right of special concern and why is it a particular threat to American institutions?

The answer is simple—perhaps even obvious. Pop art, absurd theater, pornography, the mod mode and the bearded beatnik are essentially non-fatal nuisances—minor irritations on the skin of American life in the 1960s.

The political extremism of the Radical Right and of The John Birch Society, however, is no minor surface rash on the body politic. It can be a creeping malignancy that would destroy the vital centers of the American political organism. And it is still spreading.

In the last few years, the Radical Rightist movement

helped to spark the backlash which in 1966 slowed down progress toward equal civil rights for all Americans. It is a movement which now desperately strives to keep the backlash alive. In hundreds of communities across the country, for example, the Birch Society film, *Anarchy USA*, is being shown, not to Birchite audiences alone, but to veterans groups, civic organizations and police associations, often unaware that they are watching Birch Society propaganda. The poisonous seeds are being implanted in many American minds that the just demands of Negroes for equal rights, equal justice and equal opportunity are somehow part of a worldwide Communist conspiracy—implanted in American minds already frightened and anxious over genuine Communist threats overseas.

Now the Radical Right is thrusting into new areas of public concern—insinuating itself into issues and areas vital to American national security. Radical Rightist voices are heard shrilly crying that a major American tobacco firm should not buy from Titoist Yugoslavia. Other extremist voices inveigh against a proposed consular treaty with the Soviet Union. (There may be reasonable arguments against trading with Tito or signing a consular treaty with Moscow, but the voices of the Radical Right rarely address themselves to the merits of the issues. Instead the atmosphere of public discussion of public business is polluted by shrill voices charging that trade with Tito is aid to a Communist country, asserting that a treaty with the Soviet is additional proof that the United States is governed by American traitors in high places.)

Now also the Radical Right is zeroing in on the central issue that tears at the American heart and tests the nation's capacity for steadiness and steadfastness—the war in Vietnam.

Founder Robert Welch has already sounded the trumpet call to his Birchite followers and Radical Right sympathizers for a major effort on the issue of Vietnam. Like the

219

Communists, he exploits for his own propaganda purposes and for membership recruitment the nation's continuing agony over a distasteful war.

In rallying his forces for this new effort and this new emphasis on Vietnam, Welch declared that "we have before us the most fertile ground in which to sow the seeds and nourish the plants of understanding that we have yet reached in our struggle." And he added:

> The American people are more deeply concerned about the growing mess in Vietnam—and hence more ready to pay attention to our cries of alarm—than they have been about anything else the Communist conspiracy has done to them so far.

Welch referred to the Vietnam war as a "crooked game in which all the cards are stacked against us" and as an engagement which, if not ended on terms prescribed by Welch himself, "will mark the beginning of the formal and finite end of the American Republic—exactly as the Communists in Moscow and Paris and London, and in Washington and New York, have intended that it should."

Explaining the proposed shift in Birchite emphasis from the war against the civil rights movement to Vietnam, Welch first recalled that "five years ago, few people who were thoroughly familiar with the main divisions of Communist strategy saw any chance of keeping the Negro Revolutionary Movement from reaching decisive proportions." Then he went on to say that "the required semblance of civil war which was to have been created—exactly as had been done in China and Algeria and Cuba—to help the Communists in the final stages of taking over our country, failed to materialize."

The danger of that "semblance of civil war," however, is "still with us," Welch warned his faithful followers, "because the Communists never give up in connection with any predetermined course. But today they are certainly having to bide their time a bit on this one, and their progress on this front has been slowed to a stand still."

Claiming Birch activities as a major factor in slowing down the civil rights movement, Welch pointed out that it had been accomplished by "the creation of sufficient understanding"—the Welchian euphemism for Society propaganda efforts.

In short, Welch told his members, the civil rights issue was no longer in his view as important or as urgent as it had been, and the time had come for the Society to fry other fish. And since there had been success in the civil rights area, he wrote, "who says that we cannot do an even bigger and better job in connection with the Communist strategy which revolves around the Vietnam war?"

He added:

> The stakes are even higher than in the "civil rights" fraud. The whole power of the federal government can be used, and is being used, far more openly, directly, and forcefully to support the great deception, and to stifle all opposition, than in connection even with the "civil rights" agitation.

He had, after all, long ago told the Society membership that "Washington has been taken over!"—that "Communist influences are now in working control of our Federal Government" and that "the Communists and their dupes, allies, and agents, throughout this vast apparatus of government, now actually determine almost all policies, actions, and decisions." And that was written in 1964—before the American commitment in Vietnam was increased.

In the intervening years, as has been noted, Welch told his followers that Communists were calling the shots on both sides in the Vietnam war—in Washington and in Hanoi—and that the whole American war effort was part of the larger Communist plan for taking over the United States. He expanded on these themes in a February, 1967, pamphlet called *The Truth About Vietnam* in which he

221

raised 25 invidious questions about American policy in Vietnam.

The pamphlet, obviously designed as the basic field manual for Birchite foot soldiers in the planned propaganda campaign on the Vietnam issue, set the stage not only for the Society's activities but for whatever might happen in Vietnam in the months ahead. Welch called for quick victory instead of "the long stalemate" planned by Washington. He urged the return to power of Emperor Bao Dai, an ultimatum to Hanoi and Peking that would prevent any further incursions by them in South Vietnam and which would also keep Moscow quiet, and he urged that then the United States "bring our boys home."

This shrewdly-conceived appeal to American gut reactions on Vietnam set the stage for Welch and the Birch Society to reap a propaganda harvest from the war, which Welch described as a "carefully plotted repetition of the treasonous Korean tragedy . . ."

If the progress of the war continued to be slow, the Birchers would cry that we have a treasonous "no-win" policy. If there were armistice negotiations, and especially if such talks dragged on, they would warn of sell-out by our own American representatives or claim that the United States was being hoodwinked by the Communists. If there were some sort of cease-fire or peace arrangement on anything but the conditions laid down by Founder Welch, the Birchite propaganda apparatus would cry treason, sell-out and betrayal by the Administration in Washington—charging another "Yalta," which Far Right propagandists have been denouncing since 1945. And if, by some hoped-for chance, the settlement conformed exactly to the Welchian conditions, the Birch Society would claim credit for saving the nation from planned betrayal.

The rest of the Radical Right can be expected, of course, to swing into line behind the Birchite effort to exploit the American anguish over Vietnam. It is clear, and has been for some time, that the Birch Society and its founder tend to set the tone—and to a large extent the content—of the overall Radical Rightist propaganda thrust.

There are also larger implications inherent in the Radical Rightist movement of the 1960s of which the Society is the spearhead and bellwether. These, too, make the movement a matter of special concern in the panoply of extremism on the domestic scene.

The Radical Right is a permanent fixture in American political affairs—at least in the foreseeable future. So is The John Birch Society, which has been the central factor in the flowering of the movement during the 1960s.

Whether the movement can be contained at its present strength, and whether the Birch Society can be quarantined on the fringe of the political spectrum depends in large measure on American conservatives. If they have the desire—and, more important, the will—to do the job, a housecleaning can take place on the American Right that would ostracize the Radicals. Even if the conservatives—the true conservatives—face up to their responsibility, the job will not be easy. It will also require the willingness of all Americans to recognize the danger and to accept the challenge—to realize that the penetration of American life by The John Birch Society and the Radical Right movement has already dented many communities and the political party structure itself.

The radical extremism of the movement, rooted in a conspiratorial concept of American history and of current events, threatens the democratic process and the democratic climate.

The John Birch Society claims to be the only effective anti-Communist force in the nation, but its leaders cannot tell a Republican from a Red and have forfeited all credentials and any claim whatsoever to anti-Communist expertise.

The Radical Rightist movement aids Communism by undermining public confidence in the patriotism of responsible officials, both elected and appointed, and by concentrating on a fancied internal Communist conspiracy, thus diverting public attention from real Communist threats, both internal and foreign.

The movement divides the nation by charging those who oppose it—and those whom it opposes—with being Communist dupes at best and Communist agents at worst.

It wages war against remedies seeking justice and equality for Negroes, and it seeks to exploit, for its own propaganda and recruitment purposes, the fears, the tensions, and the anxieties of Americans.

The John Birch Society aims at political influence and political power. Its ultimate purpose is to stop the forward march of American development and to repeal, if it can, the last 30 or 50 years of American history.

Birch Society members and Radical Rightist adherents have already begun to appear on the political scene. A few already hold office. More will be candidates. The Birchers and their allies bore into the vitals of our political parties.

The Birchers and their friends have penetrated and seek to influence some public agencies, such as the police, local governments and school boards.

The Birch Society seeks, through its members, influence in voluntary groups, civic organizations and other bodies which play a vital role in a free society.

The movement sucks in, each year, increasing millions of dollars for its divisive activities.

The Birch Society is an apparatus, a radical apparatus, comparable in size to the Communist apparatus at the peak of its power in the United States 20 or 25 years ago— and certainly stronger than are the Communists today.

The Society uses subterfuge and semi-secrecy—including front groups—to carry out its work.

The Birchers and their allies have excellent opportunities for continuing their growth in the years that lie immediately ahead—until their actions produce firm reactions on the part of concerned Americans, consciously convinced that the Radical Right is a menace to the nation and ready to defeat it in their own communities and in the political arena.

The Radical Rightist movement is a by-product of the fears and frustrations of a nation in transition at home and in a protracted struggle with Communism abroad—a by-product of the "long twilight struggle, year in and year out" of which the late President Kennedy spoke in his Inaugural Address.

America has rejected the false counsels of radical extremism in the past, always holding true to its best traditions—conservative in its sense of balance, liberal in its search for justice. For the American people are neither radicals nor extremists, whether or not they happen to agree with the prevailing national policies of the moment.

In the long run, Americans will also reject the false counsels of the Birchers and their allies. What is of deep concern, however, in the years ahead, is the damage that the Radical Rightist manifestation can do to the climate and the processes of democracy before the good sense and moderation of the American people render it a mere footnote in the history books of tomorrow.

Index

About the
Authors

BENJAMIN R. EPSTEIN is national director of the Anti-Defamation League of B'nai B'rith and has studied and written extensively on problems of prejudice in this country and abroad.

ARNOLD FORSTER is the League's general counsel and director of its civil rights division, and has submitted to the United States Supreme Court numerous legal briefs involving fundamental issues of civil rights.

The Radical Right: Report on the Birch Society and Its Allies is the sixth book on which Mr. Epstein and Mr. Forster have collaborated. The others are *Report on the John Birch Society 1966, The Troublemakers, Cross-Currents, Some of My Best Friends . . .* , and *Danger on the Right*. The Anti-Defamation League is one of the nation's leading organizations combating bigotry and working to strengthen the nation's democratic institutions.

323.2
E
EPSTEIN, BENJAMIN R.
   The radical Right

DATE DUE

323.2
E
EPSTEIN, BENJAMIN R.
   The radical Right

DATE DUE	BORROWER'S NAME	ROOM NUMBER
MAR 8	Ron Hadinger	
MAY 22	Renen	
OCT. 6	Nibe Englud	
MAR 2	MARK R	